DAVID R. ROSS has had a propensity his w[...]
his face in the wrong place at the wrong [...]
operating theatre for some recent constructive surgery after the latest bout of stupidity, he handed the surgeon, Mr Hammersley at Monklands Hospital, a pin up photo of a Hollywood star. Unfortunately when he woke in serious pain in the recovery room (wondering why the hell folk are vain enough to pay for that sort of exquisite agony) he found that the surgeon had not been paying attention and that he still looked like Davie Ross, only his nose was somewhat straighter than it had been since he was 14, when Jill Godley who lived up the street accidentally broke it with a kick in the wee swing park between the houses.

So he is stuck with the fact that he might look rugged, windswept and dashing in a belted plaid wearing a myriad of weaponry, but movie star good looks are, as they say in Scotland, 'oot the windae'.

Although it has been painful to pull on a crash helmet for a while, he has persevered in roaring about on his motorcycle, determined to tell the story of his country in his own particular way, and has been proud to have lived at a time when his people took their first faltering steps back to full nationhood.

James of Douglas has long been one of his heroes. He hopes you read James's story and it inspires you, and if you happen to be Scottish, that it shows you what we are capable of when we have leadership with quality.

We Scots have the honour to each have the possession of this little scrap of mountain and moorland for a lifetime. Generations have been and gone who have called themselves 'Scots'. Generations unborn will also call themselves 'Scots'. While we have the tenure of this nation, let us do these generations before and yet to come, proud, and put Scotland in her rightful place on a world stage.

Also by David R. Ross

On the Trail of Robert the Bruce
On the Trail of William Wallace
On the Trail of Bonnie Prince Charlie
On the Trail of Scotland's History
For Freedom
Desire Lines
A Passion for Scotland

James the Good
The Black Douglas

DAVID R. ROSS

Luath Press Limited
EDINBURGH
www.luath.co.uk

First published 2008

ISBN (10): 1-906307-34-2
ISBN (13): 978-1-906307-34-9

The paper used in this book is recyclable. It is made from
low chlorine pulps produced in a low energy, low emission manner
from renewable forests.

Printed and bound by
Bell & Bain Ltd., Glasgow

Typeset in 11pt Sabon by
3btype.com

Maps by Jim Lewis

Contents

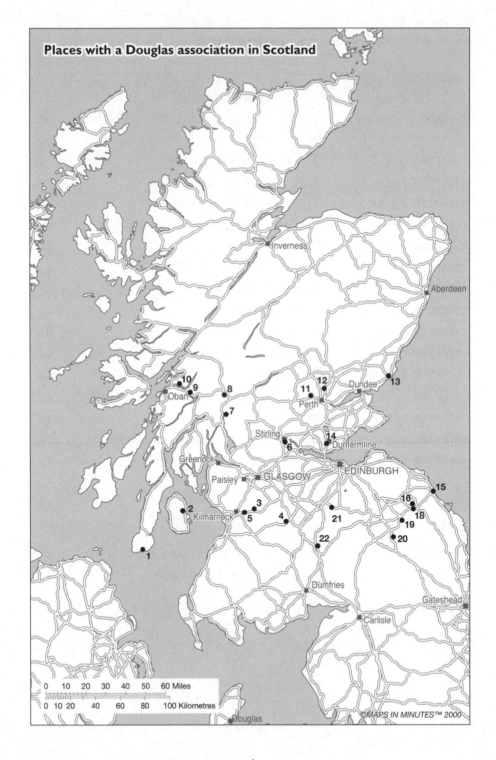

Map Key

Ref

1 Dunaverty Castle, where James took refuge with Bruce.

2 Brodick Castle. James had several adventures on the Isle of Arran.

3 Loudoun Hill. A monument on the hilltop marks the site of the battle here.

4 Douglas Castle. In the vicinity of Castle Dangerous James had many adventures. St Bride's Church, scene of the Douglas Larder and where James is buried, is nearby.

5 Hurlford. Possible site of the fight at Edryford?

6 Bannockburn. Visitor centre and rotunda mark the 1314 battle.

7 Loch Lomond, where James found the boat to ferry his companions across the loch.

8 Dail-righ. Scene of the Running Fight. The ruins of St Fillan's Chapel stand nearby.

9 The Pass of Brander. The fight against the MacDougals took place here.

10 Ardchattan Priory. James attended a council here.

11 Methven. Site of James' first major battle.

12 Scone. James attended Bruce's coronation at the Moot-hill.

13 Arbroath. Here are the ruins of the abbey which gave its name to the Declaration of 1320.

14 Dunfermline. James attended Bruce's funeral at the abbey.

15 Berwick. James had many adventures involving this Border town.

16 Skaithmuir. Scene of James' 'hardest ever fight' where he fought the Gascons in English pay.

17 Dunbar. Ruins of the castle remain where James chased the English after Bannockburn.

18 Coldstream. The English invasion began at the fords here.

19 Roxburgh Castle. Ruins remain of the castle that James stormed.

20 Lintalee. The site of James' manor house.

21 Happrew. The place where James captured Randolph from the English.

22 Arrickstane. Where James met Bruce on his way north to his coronation.

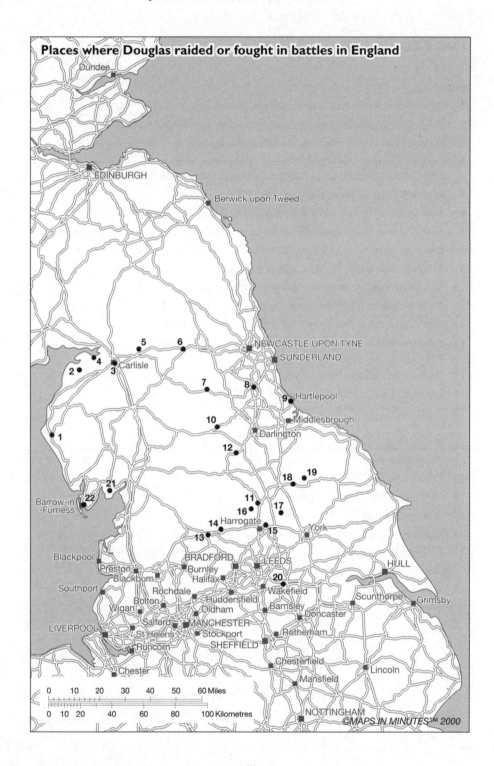

Map Key

Ref

1 Egremont. The castle ruins dominate the town.

2 Abbeytown. Holm Cultram Abbey, where the entrails of Longshanks were interred.

3 Carlisle. The Scots tried to capture the town. The castle and abbey are well worth visiting.

4 Burgh by Sands. A monument marks the place where Longshanks died.

5 Lanercost Priory. Scene of visits by the Scots.

6 Haydon Bridge, where Edward III waited in vain for the Scots.

7 Stanhope. Site of the Weardale Campaign of 1327, where the Scots humbled Edward III.

8 Durham. The Scots raided here. Its cathedral and castle survive.

9 Hartlepool. Burnt several times by Douglas. St Hilda's Church survives.

10 Barnard Castle was often subjected to raids.

11 Ripon. The population crammed into the minster for safety. Still a magnificent building.

12 Richmond. The impressive ruined castle still dominates the town.

13 Skipton. The castle is still in remarkable preservation.

14 Boulton Abbey. Ruins remain of the abbey James raided.

15 Knaresborough. The ruined castle stands high above the river.

16 Fountains Abbey. Impressive ruins remain of the church the Scots raided.

17 Myton-on-Swale. Scene of the Chapter of Myton where a scratch English army tried to attack the Scots in 1319.

18 Sutton Bank. Scene of the Battle of Byland, where the Scots defeated the English deep in their own country.

19 Rievaulx Abbey. Where Edward II narrowly missed being captured by the Scots.

20 Pontefract. One of the southernmost places the Scots reached on their raids.

21 Cartmel. The priory has survived.

22 Furness Abbey. Impressive ruins mark the scene of another Scottish raid.

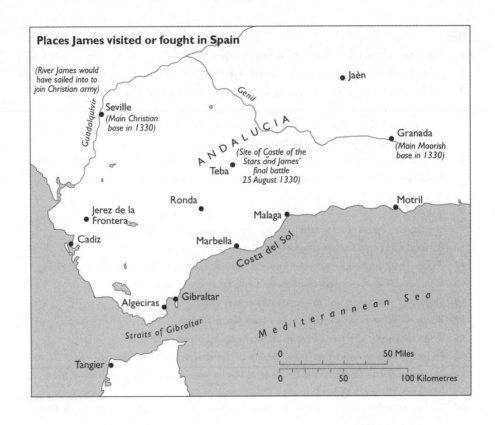

Places James visited or fought in Spain

(River James would have sailed into to join Christian army)

Guadalquivir

Genil

Jaèn

Seville
(Main Christian base in 1330)

ANDALUCIA

Granada
(Main Moorish base in 1330)

(Site of Castle of the Stars and James' final battle 25 August 1330)

Teba

Ronda

Motril

Jerez de la Frontera

Malaga

Cadiz

Marbella

Costa del Sol

Algeciras

Gibraltar

Mediterannean Sea

Straits of Gibraltar

Tangier

0   50 Miles

0   50   100 Kilometres

Preface

SIR JAMES THE GOOD, one of the finest soldiers Scotland ever produced, is better known by the name given to him by the English – the 'Black Douglas'. And they gave him this name with some justification. He terrified the northern shires of England throughout the King Robert the Bruce years of the Wars of Independence.

I feel that the people of Scotland should know more about this remarkable man, and although I wrote of him in my book *On the Trail of Robert the Bruce*, he really deserves a book dedicated solely to him.

Much of what I write of here comes from John Barbour, Archdeacon of Aberdeen (1316–1395), who wrote a great work on Robert the Bruce around 1370. He gave details of many of James Douglas's exploits in this book, allowing us an insight into the life of this remarkable man.

There is a triptych dedicated to Barbour in an aisle within St Machar's Cathedral in Aberdeen. Barbour himself is buried beneath the floor there, and a plaque to his memory is at first-floor level on the old bank building on the corner of Marischal Street and Castle Street, at the eastern end of Union Street. (I do feel that in this day and age, this name should be changed to 'Robert the Bruce Street' or similar. After all, Bruce did great things for Aberdeen, starting the common good fund and the like, and should be recognised.) Barbour's epic work on Bruce is one of the great early works of Scottish literature. I am humbled that nearly seven centuries on, I can draw on his patriotic ode, to pen one of my own.

Besides such works of literature, much of this book was of course compiled by my running around Scotland and England on my motorcycle, visiting the places that Douglas knew, and getting a feel for the way things were.

But I think it may be fitting here to quote some words of Barbour, ones I'm sure Douglas himself would wholly endorse:

A! Freedom is a noble thing!
Freedom gives man security and comfort
Freedom allows a man to be admired,
He who lives freely lives at ease!

CHAPTER ONE

The storm clouds gather

WE DO NOT KNOW the exact date on which James was born. This is not unusual for his day and age. For example, Wallace's date of birth is down to conjecture, guesswork telling us sometime between 1270 and 1274. As Robert the Bruce came from one of the leading families of Scotland, we know his birth date, 11 July 1274. But as with Wallace, we need to use what detail we have available to try and get a rough idea of when James's birth may have taken place.

His mother Elizabeth, who was a sister of James, the High Steward of Scotland (the moniker 'Steward' would soon be corrupted to 'Stewart', and that family, through marriage to Bruce's daughter, would become the ruling house of Scotland) died at the end of 1288, so obviously he must have been born before then. In 1297 he was called 'a little boy' when he was required as a hostage by the English, so his birth cannot have been too many years before his mother's death. Tradition states that James was born the same year that Alexander III, King of Scots, died, 1286, and this seems probable, or at the very least, it can't be too far away from the truth.

James was a rare name in Scotland at this time, and so it is likely that he was named after James the Steward, his uncle, who was probably his godfather.

James's likely birthplace was Douglas Castle, near Douglas village in Lanarkshire. I know kids tend to be born wherever their mother happens to be at the time, but as this castle was the family home it seems the most probable place. Only a fragment remains, standing in the old policies a mile or so east of the village. It should also be mentioned that although we tend to add second names to famous people from that time, he was actually called James 'of' Douglas, and it was not really a surname as we know it. Douglas, the village, takes its name from the nearby stream, the Dubh Glas, Gaelic for 'Black Water', which describes its sluggish dark meanderings perfectly. The locals call the village 'Dooglas', which is very close to the Gaelic pronunciation. There are now 56 towns and villages with the name Douglas across the planet, and this is the original, so the sons and daughters of this little place are far scattered.

At cliffs near Kinghorn in Fife, Alexander III, King of Scots, was fatally thrown by his horse. This began the chain of events that led to Edward I, King of England, trying to incorporate Scotland into his realm. A monument on the coast road between Burntisland and Kinghorn at Pettycur Bay marks where the body of Alexander III was discovered.

You will notice that the term used to denote a monarch in Scotland is different from that used in England. It is 'King of England', but we do not use the term 'King of Scotland' north of the Border. He was the king of his people, and monarch by their decree, hence 'King of Scots', whereas in England the power of the monarch was more absolute.

Alexander was buried in Dunfermline Abbey. The throne should have passed to Margaret, the Maid of Norway, Alexander's granddaughter, but she died in Orkney, en route to her new realm. It seems she was quite a weak, sickly child, and had suffered seasickness on the voyage over. At any rate, she died, and there was no clear heir to the throne of Scotland.

Margaret was taken back to Norway to be buried in Bergen Cathedral. The cathedral is now demolished, but a pillar marks the burial spot, and it bears Margaret's name.

There was real threat of civil war in Scotland, many of the powerful nobles having some royal blood in their veins, and all eyeing up the chance to take the ultimate step to power by assuming the crown. So, who do you get to choose a king? Who better than another king? Bishop Fraser of St Andrews wrote to the King of England, asking him to arbitrate. There was no lack of patriotism in this act. Edward was the brother-in-law of the late King Alexander, and the Scots did not see the storm clouds gathering. Scotland and England had been reasonably good neighbours and were on friendly enough terms at this point, past troubles very much forgotten. Edward came north to Norham Castle on the English side of the River Tweed to begin pondering the problem.

Although many claimants to the throne came forward, there were only two real contenders. One was John Balliol, the other Robert Bruce, grandfather of the future king. They were both close relatives of the blood royal, closer by far than the other contenders, and were also heads of leading, powerful Scottish families. English Edward chose Balliol, who did have the marginally better claim, and he ruled from 1292 to 1296.

But the English king had a hidden agenda where Scotland was concerned. Edward began to browbeat Balliol as if the latter was an underling, and Balliol went into a mutual aid alliance with France. In Scotland today, we call this alliance with France 'The Auld Alliance', as it was the start of a long relationship between the two countries, each using the other to try to counteract aggressive English inroads.

Edward was outraged. He saw Scotland as his 'sub-kingdom', and mustered his armies to teach the Scots a lesson. Using the fords at Coldstream, this invasion force crossed the River Tweed, which marks the Border of Scotland and England at the eastern side of the country. This act opened the Scottish Wars of Independence. You can stand on the strip of parkland between the town of Coldstream and the Tweed, and imagine the huge invasion force, banners flying, beginning to cross the river.

Edward marched his force east to Berwick upon Tweed, at that time the largest town in Scotland, with perhaps 18,000 inhabitants. They appeared before the town on Friday 30 March 1296.

The Dragon Banner was unfurled, which meant that there would be no mercy, no quarter given to anyone. Edward's Englishmen easily managed to breach the walls surrounding the town, and the horrific slaughter began. For three days the English killed anyone they found, regardless of age or sex. It is reported that some 15,000 lost their lives.

Apparently Edward only called his men off when he saw a woman in the act of childbirth being dragged from her home and then butchered by one of his soldiers. The Sack of Berwick is a huge stain on our history books; the most brutal slaughter ever carried out in these islands, and forever a warning to Scots of what English involvement can mean. From Berwick to the Clearances, to the closure of our industries, that involvement has never been to Scotland's weal, no matter how indoctrinated Unionists may protest otherwise.

Berwick had a strong and important castle, its site now the town's railway station, where fragments of walling remain. Probably very few of the passengers waiting to board trains from the platforms think too much about the stonework they see opposite them, but many decisions regarding Scotland's future took place within those walls. A sign above the stairs leading to the platforms tells that this was the spot where Balliol was chosen to be King of Scots, for example.

At the time of the sacking, the governor of the castle was none other than the father of James: William, Lord of Douglas. He must have seen the English army approach from the castle battlements, and was forced to watch the depredations of the English from its walls.

Douglas and his men would have known that there was no way they could be relieved from their plight, trapped inside the castle, having no doubt that the victorious and bloodthirsty English would soon find a way in.

The garrison of the castle surrendered on terms, and William Douglas was taken north with Edward as he marched his army over the land of Scotland to show who was now in charge.

The Scots did mount a resistance, of course. Their feudal host gathered at Caddonlea, near the village of Caddonfoot, upstream on the Tweed. They caught up with the English invaders as they were besieging the castle of Dunbar while advancing up the east coast. The garrison of the castle took heart from the appearance of the Scottish army, and began to taunt the besiegers with cries of 'Tailed dogs! We will cut your tails off!' This was because the Scots constantly related the story that Englishmen had tails that they kept tucked away hidden in their trousers. It was said that some Englishmen had dishonoured a holy man (variously cited to be Thomas à Becket or St Augustine) and so God had given them tails to their everlasting shame. I don't think that the Scots truly believed this, but it was a suitable stick to beat Englishmen with, and it did seem to enrage them.

On Friday 27 April 1296, the two armies clashed in the fields above the Spott Burn, and the Scots were, quite frankly, far outclassed and cut to pieces. William Douglas would have been forced to watch this from a distance, and must have despaired at the twist of fate that was befalling Scotland at this time.

I have often wondered if William Wallace was present at the battle of Dunbar. If so, although escaping with his life unlike so many of his fellow countrymen, he got a hard lesson on the power of the English army in the field. Certainly, his future co-commander at the battle of Stirling Bridge, Andrew Murray, was captured here, but was later able to escape from his prison at Chester and make his way north to raise his clansmen.

Medieval warfare had rules of a sort, and losers were expected to acknowledge the fact in a gentlemanly way. It would take Wallace's, Bruce's and then Douglas's example to finally erase this notion from the minds of Scots, and let them see that there should be no rules when it came to freeing your country from the grasp of an aggressor.

Edward marched ever further north. The Steward surrendered Roxburgh Castle, Edinburgh held out for a week, and Stirling Castle was merely abandoned. John Balliol, King of Scots, was captured and brought before Edward at Stracathro Kirk near Brechin. A new plaque on the churchyard wall commemorates this. He was humiliated, having his crown and lion rampant surcoat torn from him. He was taken south to the Tower of London, and then exiled to his family lands in France. Ordinary Scots were slain out of hand by Edward, but he saw Balliol as part of the feudal mechanism that supported his own style of life, and so treated him in a more lenient fashion.

Edward then turned his attention to 'asset stripping' Scotland. He looted the crown jewels, and all the plate and jewellery he could find in Edinburgh, and sent it all south. But the greatest loss to the Scottish people was Edward's removal of our historical records. A nation is a result of its shared history, and Edward tried to destroy ours. He took the Holy Rood of St Margaret, the country's most precious relic, and had it sent to London too. 'Rood' is the old Scots for 'cross', and this venerated item was believed to be a piece of the True Cross on which Christ was crucified. Holyrood Abbey was built to accommodate this relic, hence its name. It has been an important place to the people of Scotland over the centuries, and still is today. Holyrood Palace, built alongside the old abbey, was the favourite residence of many kings of Scots, and the modern Scottish Parliament building is usually just called 'Holyrood' by the media.

When Edward reached Perth, he commanded that the Stone of Destiny be taken from nearby Scone Abbey, and that it too be sent to England's capital, as an offering to Edward the Confessor. It was to remain in his chapel inside Westminster Abbey for seven centuries, before it was rightfully returned to Scotland.

The Stone is supposedly Jacob's Pillow from the Bible, brought from North Africa by the people who first made Scotland their home, and an old legend states that wherever the Stone is found, from there the

Scots shall be ruled. It was returned to Scotland in 1996 to go on display in Edinburgh Castle, and a year later the Scots voted for a parliament of sorts again, also in Edinburgh, so the old legend has proven true! There has been much debate over the last century whether the Stone that was looted by Edward was the 'real' Stone, or whether he took a fake that was substituted by the monks at Scone. As this is all down to supposition and as there is no concrete evidence to back up such claims, we have to assume that the Stone currently in Edinburgh is the true Stone.

When English Edward crossed the Border south again, we do not really know what had become of William Douglas, James's father. He had somehow been removed from Edward's retinue. His movements over the next few months are unrecorded. When Wallace began his career in May 1297, after slaughtering Heselrig, the English sheriff of Lanark, he struck north and made a raid on Scone, hoping to capture or kill the English-appointed justiciar of Scotland, William Ormsby. William Douglas joined him on this raid. In fact, Douglas was one of the few noblemen who joined Wallace's desperados in the early days. Ormsby barely escaped with his life, jumping out of a window as the Scots came through the door, leaving all his valuables behind.

William Douglas has left a reputation for wildness and recklessness behind him. After the death of his wife Elizabeth Stewart (James's mother) in 1288, he abducted and forcibly married Eleanor Ferrers, an English widow, while she was visiting relatives in Scotland. As she was an English noblewoman, the matter was brought to the attention of King Edward, who was not best pleased with Douglas's actions. Douglas had carried out executions without consulting the proper authorities in Scotland, and it seems he could be very difficult to deal with. His aggression probably suited the early days of Wallace's campaign.

What is more surprising is that the 22-year-old Robert Bruce, future King of Scots, joined Wallace's band. He had been a favourite of King Edward, but suddenly joined his fellow countrymen. The *Chronicle of Guisborough* states that he 'joined the Scots because he was a Scot'. Surely a simple enough explanation?

Bruce had to have an excuse to amass his men, and one came when he was asked by the English to mount a raid on Douglasdale. When they reached the walls of Douglas Castle, Bruce suddenly changed his allegiance. He carried those within Douglas Castle to safety, among whom is likely to have been the young James, then about 11 years of age. Neither James nor Robert would have guessed what fate had in store for them both – how their lives would be intertwined in the fateful struggle for the freedom of their nation.

On 11 September 1297, the battle of Stirling Bridge took place. Wallace and Murray, against all odds, defeated an English army as it tried to cross the River Forth. Unfortunately Murray received wounds that were to kill him later in the year. Wallace went on to invade England. The following year Edward of England came north, leading his army in person. He clashed with Wallace and the Scots at Falkirk on 22 July 1298. Woodend Farm near the Westquarter Burn marks the site of the Scots' positions. A new commemorative cairn in the grounds of Callendar House in Falkirk has been raised in memory of this battle. The Scots were defeated with heavy losses. Wallace went back to fighting a guerrilla campaign, and then went abroad to France and Italy to try and elicit help for Scotland's cause.

I can imagine the news of these events being carried across Scotland by word of mouth, and the young James hearing of them. He was a patriot, bred to be a leader of men. How did his emotions cope with these reports of the resistance of his countrymen? Did he long to be of an age where he was able to take the field on Scotland's behalf? At some point during these campaigns James ended up living in Paris. Barbour tells us that when James's father was eventually captured by the English and led south to the Tower of London in chains, his lands given over to the English Lord Clifford, James was left without his inheritance. Whether he was sent by members of his family to prevent him being taken hostage by the English, or whether he travelled on a whim looking for adventure, James did indeed move to France. Barbour tells us he lived simply, sometimes in ribald company, and that he learned much of life in the Parisian streets. I can imagine him there, gazing up at the towers of the Cathedral of Notre Dame, still under construction, or pausing to look into the depths of the River Seine.

We are told that he spent a total of three years in the French capital. During this sojourn came the fateful day when a messenger came looking for him, bearing ill news. His father, William Douglas, was dead.

Barbour tells us that he was murdered by the English while a prisoner in chains in the Tower of London. James swore there and then that he would do all in his power to recover all that had been his father's; that he would dedicate his life to redeeming his inheritance.

He travelled back to Scotland and made contact with Bishop Lamberton of St Andrews in Fife. Lamberton is known to have been a great patriot in the Scottish cause, but he came to English peace when it suited him and Scotland best. He had the ear of English officials, but we know he entered into a secret bond to push the claim of the future King Robert around this time. James, like a young page, was given the job of waiting on Lamberton at table.

Barbour tells us, 'all men loved him for his nobleness, for he was of the most fair demeanour, wise, courteous, and debonair. He was liberal and kind also, and above all things loved loyalty.'

King Edward came north in 1304 to hold an assembly at Stirling. Lamberton saw this as an opportunity to get James back into a situation where he might have some claim to his family lands. James was perhaps 18 at the time of this incident.

Lamberton led him into an audience with Edward and said, 'Sir, I bring you this child, who seeks to be your man, and prays of your grace to receive here his homage and grant him his inheritance.' Edward asked, what lands did he claim? Lamberton informed him that he claimed the lordship of Douglas, and that he was the son of the late William. Edward was notorious for his fits of temper, and men had died at his whim. He rose from his chair, becoming enraged. Lamberton knew that look well, and knew to tread warily. The king seemed preoccupied with the fact that William Douglas had joined forces with Wallace, whom he hated with a passion. He told Lamberton, 'His father was ever my cruel foe, and died for it in my prison. He was against my majesty, therefore I am entitled to be his heir.' Lamberton hastened James away from Edward's presence, fearing his cruelty.

King Edward did not realise that he had cast a die in this meeting. In the words of the writer I. M. Davis, 'The Hammer of the Scots watched them go, unaware that he had just dismissed the future Hammerer of the English.'

CHAPTER TWO

Experiments in chivalry

AFTER THE DISMISSAL by Edward I, James, more determined than ever to get back all that had been taken from his family by the English invaders, must have fretted as to how he could put his dreams into action. News of the national situation would now and again filter through to his ears.

Wallace was eventually captured by the English, and suffered a most horrific death in London. He was forced to endure a mockery of a trial on the morning of 23 August 1305 in Westminster Hall. From there he was hauled out, tied to the tails of horses, and dragged through London's streets for six miles. He was hanged, cut down while still alive, then disembowelled. His heart was torn out, ending his life, and his innards were taken out and burned. His body was quartered, his head spiked on London Bridge, and his body parts distributed over Scotland to warn the Scots not to try to withstand English rule. James must have heard about this and despaired for Scotland. We don't know if James and Wallace ever met, but it is possible, as James's father and Wallace campaigned together. Lamberton too was a great supporter and backer of Wallace, and it is possible that they had meetings while James was present.

It took two years from James's dismissal by Edward for fate to take a hand. During that time James continued his duties with Lamberton at St Andrews. He must have daydreamed. Wondering. Wondering; 'I am one man, what can I do to instigate action?' Then one day, news arrived. Lamberton received a letter telling of deeds that had happened in Dumfries.

Robert the Bruce knew that if the struggle against English rule was to be continued, drastic action had to be taken. First his grandfather – the competitor for the throne against Balliol – and then his father had died. Bruce knew that he had inherited a valid claim to be king. He approached John Comyn, the nephew of John Balliol, head of that faction since

Balliol's exile, and offered him the Bruce lands if Comyn would back Bruce's claim to Scotland's throne. Comyn agreed. A mutual pact was signed. But Comyn went to English Edward and showed him the letter with Bruce's seal attached.

King Edward summoned Bruce. At that time Bruce was in Edward's peace and was in London, and Edward confronted him with the letter. Bruce stated that he was not sure that the attached seal was indeed his, and that it could well be a forgery. That night, Bruce, accompanied by a clerk, rode away secretly for Scotland.

Bruce had made his escape, knowing that Comyn had betrayed him, but also knowing that he had no way back into leading a quiet life. King Edward knew Bruce had plotted against him, and he would now kill Bruce if he could.

A tale has come down to us that the English Earl of Gloucester tried to warn Bruce that he had been betrayed. He sent Bruce money and a pair of spurs as a strong hint to flee.

No matter, Bruce knew that he was undone. Five days later he crossed the Border, only to find that Comyn was at nearby Dumfries. The two men came face to face before the high altar of the Greyfriars Monastery there on 10 February 1306. Bruce accused Comyn of trying to instigate his betrayal. Hot words were exchanged and daggers were drawn. Bruce stabbed Comyn. A heinous act, Comyn's blood splashing against the altar. Sacrilege.

Bruce staggered outside, and when his men gathered round to ask what had happened, Bruce replied, 'I doubt I have slain the Comyn!' Sir Roger Kirkpatrick of Closeburn, one of Bruce's staunchest adherents, replied, 'You doubt? I'll mak siccar!' (Scots for 'I'll make sure'). He ran into the church, and finished off the badly wounded Comyn. Comyn's uncle was also slain in the ensuing fracas. The motto of the Kirkpatrick family has ever since been 'I'll mak siccar'.

A plaque in Dumfries's Burns Square marks the site of the Greyfriars Monastery where this act took place. When building work was taking place there in the late 1800s, the site of the high altar was discovered, with the graves of churchmen to one side. At the opposite side, two skeletons in armour were found. It seems these may be the bodies of Comyn and his uncle. Bruce could not very well have sent them back to Comyn's family after what took place there, so they must have been hastily buried. The shops on either side of the plaque do not have cellars as the remains were left intact and simply bricked over. So when you are in Burns Square you are actually standing above the last resting place of Comyn!

Bruce knew there was no way back. For better or worse, there was only one route to take. He and his ran to quickly capture the Castle of Dumfries. They tore down the standard flying the three crouching leopards of England, and hurriedly ran up the lion rampant of Scotland. Bruce declared to the astonished townsfolk that he was to become their king.

Greyfriars Church, just a few yards from the plaque on the other side of the square, was the site of the castle there, although there are large earthworks of another castle in the town's Castledykes Park, and a plaque there proclaims it to be the one that Bruce took.

Bruce was no fool; he knew that trouble was ahead. Word of the slaying of the Comyn at the altar would be conveyed to the Pope, and he knew that he would be excommunicated. This would mean that he would be unable to go through the crowning ceremony, due to the religious restrictions involved. He knew that he had to move quickly to progress to Scone, where by tradition, all Kings of Scots were crowned. This had to be done with haste before word could be carried to Rome.

As the story unfolded before Lamberton, James realised that the time for action had come. He approached Lamberton and told him that he wished to join Bruce and take his chances. He could not hope to regain his lands unless the English were expelled, and obviously Bruce was going to attempt to expel them. Although a churchman, and though news of the stabbing at the altar must have worried him, Lamberton knew that Scotland must come first in all this, and he endorsed James's going to Bruce and joining the men now gathering to his standard. But he could not let the English know that he approved of such a course of action.

He outlined a plan to James. Lamberton had a good horse in his stables. Barbour even tells us the name of this horse: Ferrand. Lamberton gave James some money, and instructions to take the horse and ride off with it as though stealing it and absconding. Lamberton knew that the groom in the stables would try to stop James, and his evidence would make the English believe in the ruse. James made his way to the stables and began to saddle Ferrand. The groom did indeed get into a fight with James, trying to stop him. James struck the man down, and managed to gallop off into the night. He was determined to make contact with Bruce and offer his services.

Bruce and his retinue made their way north towards Scone and the impending coronation. They headed north up Annandale, Bruce's ancestral family lands, where men could flock to his standard en route. Annandale is the valley, or dale, of the River Annan. Passing the town of Moffat, the cavalcade made its way towards the Devil's Beef Tub, a huge natural feature shaped like a bowl, where Borderers were apt to secrete stolen cattle. An old Roman road rose over a shoulder of the Beef Tub, crossing the intervening hills to Clydesdale. They could then follow the River Clyde towards Glasgow, and strike over the Lowlands for Perth and nearby Scone. As they started to climb into the hills, some horsemen were spotted ahead, obviously waiting for them. It was James with a group of riders, probably some of his own followers, as Douglasdale was not far distant from there.

They met at the Arrickstane. I assume there was a large boulder of that name on the hillside at one time. It is still marked on maps, but there does not seem to be anything prominent enough to merit such recognition. The name survives today in the farm of Ericstone in the glen below. The view out from Arrickstane is a magnificent one, the Lake District hills in the north of England visible to the south, and all Annandale stretching away below. I find it a touching place to stand, imagining those two great heroes of Scotland beginning an adventure that writers of fiction could not match. An adventure that would end 24 years later in Mediterranean climes. Douglas knew that Bruce would come that way north, and it was an obvious place to wait and look for riders approaching from the south.

As Bruce drew up, James dismounted and knelt before him. He swore to be his true man, and gave his fealty. Bruce pulled him up, and told the young man he was happy to have him join his followers. But at this point James was green and untried, and could not have been accounted much of a catch. He would have fallen in at the rear of the cavalcade, but was probably happy that he was making that first step to the recovery of his heritage.

Bruce was crowned on the Moot Hill at Scone on Friday 25 March

1306. There the kings of Scots had been crowned since time immemorial. Several earls of Scotland were in attendance, as well as many of the lairdly class. The Moot Hill is a raised piece of ground, and it was there the Stone of Destiny used to sit. Scone Abbey was nearby, but it, alas, is long gone, destroyed during the Reformation, when Protestantism replaced Catholicism. It was fired by the mob in 1559. The old grave-yard survives, but there is nothing of real antiquity there. A small chapel also survives on the Moot Hill, but it is from a later building, con-structed in 1624.

How I would love it if I could go and visit the old abbeys of Scotland intact, as nearly all are in ruins today. I would love to have seen the inte-rior of the abbey, as such a large part of Scotland's destiny was shaped there, and it also contained the tomb of Robert II, Bruce's grandson.

Bishop Wishart of Glasgow lowered the crown onto Bruce's head. The Earl of Fife, the foremost earl of Scotland, normally carried out the crowning ceremony, but the current representative was very much in the pocket of Edward. However, after the ceremony was over, Fife's aunt Isobel, Countess of Buchan, appeared. She had hoped to be there in time to place the crown on Bruce's head, and was tearful that she had missed the opportunity to do her duty. Bruce, a warrior, but a man who was to show great compassion throughout his career, held a second coronation two days after the first. Isobel's journey had not been in vain.

Unfortunately, Edward of England would soon exact a terrible vengeance on Isobel for her patriotism.

James would have been among the onlookers, watching as the circlet of gold was lowered onto Bruce's brow. For better or worse, both his and Bruce's fates were in place. Edward of England would soon be appraised of the deeds that had taken place there, and his rage would be great. Bruce's wife Elizabeth was now Queen of Scots, and she is reported to have said after the ceremony to her husband that 'they were but King and Queen of the May'. By this she meant that what they were doing might be no more than a children's game. Edward would be determined to spoil the party, and more likely sooner than later.

On 5 April 1306, King Edward appointed Aymer de Valence as his lieu-tenant in Scotland. He gave him power to 'Raise Dragon'. Like the Dragon Banner unfurled before Berwick, this meant that the Valence could slay without any comeback. De Valence was a cousin of King Edward. He was also brother-in-law of the murdered Comyn, and so he intended to hunt Bruce down with all his power. He had Lamberton sent south to England in irons. He also captured Bishop Wishart of Glasgow, who suffered a similar fate. Poor Wishart was never to see his beloved Scotland again. When he was finally released after Bannockburn in 1314, he was blind. His defaced tomb is at the rear of Glasgow Cathedral, unmarked and uncared for, surrounded by the Union flags of regiments of the British Army. A situation that needs to be rectified.

De Valence took up quarters in the walled city of Perth.

On 18 June 1306, Bruce appeared before the city walls with the men who had mustered to him since his coronation, now a small army. He challenged de Valence to either surrender the town or come out and fight. De Valence had his herald announce that, as it was a Sunday, he declined to fight. But if Bruce were to return on the morrow, he would oblige him. Bruce took him at his word and retired west a few miles to Methven, where his men could camp. They were sited in the ground just to the east of Methven Castle, a later version of which stands in the vicinity today.

As Bruce's men, James included, were cooking or settling down for the night, their swords and armour discarded, de Valence suddenly attacked. Some Scots managed to organise a piecemeal defence, but it quickly turned into a rout. Bruce escaped by the skin of his teeth. His nephew, Thomas Randolph, was captured. Unlikely as it must have seemed at the time, the futures of Randolph and James were soon to be entwined. Sixteen other captured gentlemen of knightly rank were not so lucky. Edward had them executed at Newcastle in northern England. One of these was Alexander Scrymgeour, the hereditary standard bearer of the battle army of Scotland. He had carried the banner for Wallace, and suffered the same horrible fate as the latter, being disembowelled before his heart was torn out. They were friends from school in Dundee, and Wallace had made Scrymgeour his standard bearer. He valiantly carried the lion rampant banner behind Wallace at Falkirk, and Bruce, after being crowned, gave the royal stamp of approval to Wallace's appointment, making Scrymgeour's position hereditary.

James, along with his king, managed to make his escape. The fragments of the army gathered and headed east, sorely depleted. Bruce swore that he would never trust the word of an Englishman again. He had tried to conduct himself within the laws of chivalry, fighting fairly, and de Valence had used underhand tactics. James was privy to this, and although he had been raised as the son and heir of a great lord, he was schooled in a hard lesson at Methven. If the English used lies and deceit to wage war, he would become a master in that field. The learning process that was to make him one of the greatest soldiers Scotland would ever produce had begun. Little did Bruce know in that time of despair, that one of his lowly captains would soon show a great flair for terrorising the invaders of his country.

CHAPTER THREE

The slow climb to success

BRUCE AND THE REMNANTS of his army headed west, James somewhere among them. They went by the Abbey of Inchaffray. 'Inch' is the Scots word for 'island', and the abbey once stood in very boggy marshland. All that remains today is one gable-end wall, a vaulted chamber and a scattering of stonework.

Abbot Maurice of Inchaffray was one of Bruce's most trusted advisors. He was lucky in his churchmen; Lamberton, Wishart et al. Good Scots every one. And more would appear throughout the campaign for Independence, with the particular skills that suited the immediate need.

Abbot Maurice guided Bruce and his followers west along Loch Earn side. From there they turned north into Glen Ogle, and then dropped into Glen Dochart.

Bruce's route after Methven is reasonably well documented. But I should point out here that, much further north, there is a plaque set into the gable wall of a ruined cottage. It reads:

Collebhrochain.
Robert the Bruce
Rested here after
The Battle of Methven.

This cottage stands in a field adjacent to woodland, to the south of the B8019, just after it crosses the River Garry north west of Pitlochry. Perhaps Bruce was there at a later point in his career, and the legend has stuck, but it is very doubtful that he was there after Methven.

In Glen Dochart Bruce hoped to find respite, and he got some at the shrine of St Fillan, the ruins of which stand on the east side of the River Fillan, midway between Crianlarich and Tyndrum, by the West Highland Way.

The holy men there gave Bruce and his followers their blessings, and Bruce was to return this favour in various grants he made to them over the next few years. Relics of St Fillan, a bell and a crozier – the ornate curved top-piece of a bishop's staff – are on display at the Museum of Scotland in Edinburgh.

James must have looked out at the unfamiliar Highland landscape, to the high hills like Ben More and Stobinian, or west to Ben Lui, and found it higher and rockier by far than the gentle rolling hills of Douglasdale.

It was not long before Bruce's enemies discovered his whereabouts. John McDougall of Lorne, a cousin of the murdered Comyn, suddenly assailed Bruce at a spot a little south of Tyndrum. Bruce's men had to fight a sharp rearguard action to escape with their lives. James again survived. Perhaps the natural ability he had in the field of battle was beginning to tell. He managed to cut his way out of the ambush, but not untouched; Barbour tells us that James was wounded in the fight. He does not give us any more detail about how badly James was injured, but it could not have been too serious as it does not seem to have impaired his progress in any way. Nonetheless, he certainly received his first battle wound in this encounter. Bruce had a narrow escape. He was assailed by three of McDougall's clansmen, but was the master of the battle-axe, and used it with murderous effect, dispatching all three of his assailants. One man, falling backwards, was left with Bruce's brooch in his hand. This brooch is still in the possession of the McDougalls of Dunollie. It contains a large crystal surrounded by eight pearls. The centre section unscrews and presumably held a relic or memento of some sort.

The site of this battle has since been known as Dail-Righ, Gaelic for 'King's Field', which is the name of the farm there. The modern version of this name is Dal-Righ (pronounced 'Dal-ree'). Driving north towards Tyndrum on the A82, the farm of Dal-Righ is signposted. If you drive up the entrance road, you will see that there is a parking area a few yards on to your left. There is a modern standing stone there giving local information, and one snippet concerns the fight. It states:

> The Battle of Dalrigh in 1306. Robert the Bruce and his men, who were being pursued [it actually says 'pursed' on the inscription!] by McDougall of Lorne threw their heaviest weapons into a

small lochan. They were caught at Dalrigh, but killed McDougall's men and escaped.

I have heard this story of Bruce and his men discarding some of their weapons to try and escape their pursuers, but I think that it may just be local legend. I am unaware of any weapons found in this vicinity.

Tradition asserts that Bruce and his men found some relief by retreating to a castle that stood on an island in Loch Dochart. The ruins that can be seen from the roadside today are of a later structure, built by Sir Duncan Campbell sometime between 1585 and 1631.

Barbour tells us that James started to stand out a little at this time. He had a flair for hunting, and more than any other in Bruce's party, excelled at finding food for the pot.

Bruce's womenfolk, who had been at his coronation, then at the camp at Methven, had managed to escape and were still with him. We are told that they were very complimentary to the young James regarding his hunting and trapping abilities. We can be sure that the young man was flattered by their attentions. Meanwhile, Bruce was aware that he had many enemies: not just the English, but also the many branches of the Comyn family, as well as Scots who just did not want Bruce as their king. It must have seemed that there was nowhere really safe for him in Scotland, and that every man's hand was turned against him. In light of this, Bruce decided that he had to send the women away. The Earl of Atholl, who was older than most of the party, and who was struggling after all the alarms and travelling he had been through, was to leave with the ladies. After some debate, it was decided to split the surviving group in two. Atholl and the ladies, including Bruce's queen and his daughter, were to be escorted by Bruce's brother Nigel and one of his staunchest supporters, Robert Boyd, as well as a section of the troops. They were to set off to the north east, heading for Kildrummy Castle in upper Donside in Aberdeenshire. Kildrummy still stands. It is ruined, but the outline is more or less complete, comprising four round towers, a hall and a chapel. It is in the care of Historic Scotland and is open to visitors.

The women and their escort were besieged at Kildrummy. The castle was strong and well provisioned and could have held out a long time, but a traitor in their midst set fire to the stables and they were forced to abandon the place and head north. It has been assumed that the party was intending to try and find a ship for Orkney or even Norway, where they would be among friends. Unfortunately, they were betrayed again at St Duthac's Chapel at Tain in Ross-shire. (The remnants stand in the graveyard there.) King Edward had the menfolk horribly executed. The tired old Earl of Atholl was hanged from an exceptionally high gallows, then beheaded and burned. Nigel, Bruce's brother, was drawn, hanged and beheaded.

To be drawn meant to be dragged to the place of execution behind horses. In fact, King Edward's violence and ferocity towards Scots stepped up a gear around this point, inflicting many disembowelments and similarly unspeakable, agonising deaths. But most shocking at the time was his treatment of Bruce's women.

In those days of chivalry, respect for women was the norm. Edward confined Bruce's queen, Elizabeth, in the manor house at Burstwick in Holderness in eastern England. Christian, Bruce's sister, was confined in a nunnery at Sixhills in Lincolnshire. Her husband, Christopher Seaton, had been disembowelled on an eminence in Dumfries called the Crystal Mount; the site is crowned by St Mary's Church today. Both these ladies had no access to everyday life, and were allowed to talk to no one. Bruce's other sister Mary was imprisoned in a cage of wood and iron and hung over the walls of Roxburgh Castle. Isobel, Countess of Buchan, who had crowned Bruce, was kept in a similar cage at Berwick. These women were left in their cages in all weathers, with no privacy, for all to gaze upon like animals in a zoo. Edward also ordered that Bruce's daughter Marjory, only 12, was to be kept in a cage in the Tower of London, with access to no one. Edward's own advisors thought this too much, and he revoked this savagery, and she was confined instead at the Gilbertine Nunnery at Watton in Yorkshire. It was only after Bruce's decisive victory at Bannockburn in 1314 that he was able to use English prisoners to ransom these women's release.

I mention the places of confinement of these women deliberately, as the locations of the chosen spots are interesting. They were all on the Border, or just a little deeper into England in the cases of Bruce's queen and daughter. Perhaps this was to make the Scots raid south to try and assay their release, and in so doing take just a little too much of a risk.

James was, in the coming years, to make endless forays into northern England. He must have planned and schemed many times, wondering if the release of these women could be carried off. But, of course, they were all sited where Scots attempting a rescue could easily be cut off and annihilated.

Meanwhile, Bruce, knowing nothing of the fate of his ladies and friends, headed into the south west, looking for a friendlier environment in which to regather his fighting strength. Kintyre was his first goal, then perhaps Ireland. He had a force of roughly 200. James went with him too, of course.

They travelled down Glen Falloch, local legend telling us that they hid out at Clach nam Breatann, the 'Stone of the Britons', near the south end of the glen. This was an ancient boundary stone, marking the northern limit of the kingdom of the Strathclyde Britons.

One of the king's most trusted lieutenants, Neil Campbell, whose loyalty during these campaigns was to result in grants of land that would begin the expansion of his family's power, was sent on ahead to his clan lands to try and gather some manpower and to organise shipping.

Due to the proximity of hostile enemies, Bruce's band made their way down the eastern side of Loch Lomond. Barbour tells us that Bruce worried greatly about his men, as they had to lie on open hillsides during long nights, some of them unable to sleep. The year was passing, and the nights were growing cold.

Bruce's men were operating very much on trust. He had been defeated in battle at Methven and had had to mount a sharp retreat at Dail-Righ. James, at 20 years of age, was young and tough, and does not seem to have had a problem with the adventures at hand.

There is a cave at Craigroyston still pointed out as one where Bruce's men lurked. Their enemies had made sure that there were no boats that they could use left along the many miles of loch shore. But James at last found a little sunken rowboat, probably just scuppered by its owner so that he could retrieve it later. James managed to drag it to shore and tip out the water. He discovered that it was intact, and happily went back to Bruce to tell him of his find. It could only hold three people, and the first trip across to the comparative safety of the opposite shore comprised Bruce, James and an oarsman.

The oarsman dropped them on the west shore and went back to bring over another two. Barbour tells us that it took a day and a night of to-ing and fro-ing to get everyone to the far side. Some of the party elected to swim, hanging on to the boat. And having swum in Loch Lomond, I can assure you that any time of the year, the water is chilly to say the least!

We are told that Bruce recited an old romance, that of Fierabras, to his men to amuse them as they sat waiting for the little boat to disgorge another couple of their companions to the western shore. James must have been one of the sitters, listening to the tales told by his king.

They were in dire need of food, and two parties went out foraging, one led by Bruce, the other by James, who had already proved his worth in this field, and was now being given little positions of power. While out, they encountered Malcolm, the Earl of Lennox, who was overjoyed to meet his friend Bruce, and furnished them with food and supplies.

From there, Malcolm led them to the Firth of Clyde, and they again encountered Neil Campbell, who had kept his word and gathered up as many sailing craft as he could from his clan lands. They set sail, keeping near the shore as they passed the island of Bute, as hugging the land would make them harder to spot for ships out at sea. For some reason Malcolm's galley fell behind the rest of the little fleet, and traitors from Bute tried to overtake his ship. Malcolm threw much of his gear overboard, and his pursuers, eager for plunder, fell upon it and gave up the chase. Malcolm caught the rest of the fleet at the castle of Dunaverty, on the Kintyre peninsula.

Bruce, James and the rest of the men accepted the hospitality of Angus Og, Lord of the Isles, whose stronghold Dunaverty was. It stood on a cliff-girt rock jutting into the sea at the south of the Kintyre peninsula, some 10 miles south of Campbeltown. Only minor fragments remain. The site of Dunaverty is accessible from the cottage that stands alongside, but extreme care should be taken on its uneven grassy top as it is a fair old drop to the sea, boiling and bubbling on the rocks below.

A massacre took place at Dunaverty in the 1600s, and the unfortunate victims were buried in the little walled enclosure in the field between the castle site and the B842.

Bruce's party stayed at Dunaverty for three days, then made its way across to the island of Rathlin, just off the Irish coast, Scotland and Ireland being only a few miles apart at that point. The English were strong in shipping, and had a fleet based in the area, and as Rathlin could be assailed easily, we must surmise that Bruce did not stay there too long.

Historians have always debated where Bruce spent the winter of 1306–07. Barbour only mentions Rathlin, but it is more likely that Bruce travelled round some of the Western Isles, perhaps as far north as the area of Ardnamurchan. James of course accompanied his king on these travels. He must have absorbed all that he saw; the way the clans operated, travelling by longship and galley, water being the easiest way to journey that savage seaboard. Not to mention that he must have been taken aback at the extraordinary scenery of that part of Scotland.

It seems Bruce did manage to send someone over to his family lands in Ayrshire to collect some of the rents that were due to him, and he would have used this money to hire as many fighting men as he could. This, coupled with his family ties in Ireland and the Hebrides, would have given him a fighting force ready to be used when the winter turned to spring in early 1307.

Barbour tells us that James was beginning to fret as winter went on, feeling that wild weather should not stop him from trying to expel the invader from Scotland. He had a talk with another of Bruce's captains, Robert Boyd. He suggested they could take some men and assail Brodick Castle on the Isle of Arran in the Firth of Clyde. Boyd knew Arran well, and agreed to the plan. They approached Bruce and asked to be allowed to try and carry this out. He gave them leave to do so. This shows that James had gone up greatly in Bruce's esteem, as he was still only aged 20 or 21 and was being put in a position of trust.

They got together a small force and rowed over to Arran from Kintyre, landing in the dead of night. They secreted the boat, all its gear and tackle being hidden in bushes, then crept up to the castle before the sky started to lighten. The Englishman in charge at Brodick was Sir John Hastings. James had heard that Hastings often rode out with his followers on forays round the island, and made ready to way-lay him the next time he did so. But as they sat there in readiness for ambush, three English ships appeared laden with provisions, clothing and arms for the castle garrison. A body of men started to unload the boats, and as they strolled by the Scots, carrying barrels of wine and other victuals, James and his men broke cover and attacked them boldly. They slew around 40, and the ensuing cries and screams roused the castle. The garrison sallied out to take on James's band, and his men, nothing loath, turned to meet them. The English did not expect such a ferocious assault. They probably thought that they would be assailing some disgruntled locals, and they soon fell back in confusion, beginning to run for the castle gates. James's men cut down everyone they could overtake, but the castle gates were barred against them.

They turned again and made for the three ships, whose crews had quickly put to sea when they saw that their comrades break and run at the Scots' assault. But a contrary wind had risen and they could not get past the breakers to put to the open sea. They were trapped there, unable to land for fear of the Scots. Eventually two of the ships took on so much water that they capsized. The Scots, jubilant, gathered up what they could and made their way to a place where they felt they could mount a defence against any reprisals by the English, happy with the amount of plunder they had amassed.

There is a spot at the head of Glen Cloy containing earthworks that are claimed to be the remains of James's camp. Certainly the *Gazetteer of Scotland* I have for the year 1830 tells that Bruce granted the estate of Kilmichael in Glen Gloy to a family named Fullarton, for services rendered. It adds that the then owner still retained his original charter from Bruce, dated 26 November 1307.

James and Robert Boyd remained there 10 days. Bruce meanwhile had arrived at Arran with 33 galleys, and made enquires to which area of the island James had retired. Bruce made his way to Glen Cloy and blew a blast on his horn. James and Robert Boyd both recognised it to be the note of Bruce's own, and they emerged to tell Bruce of their adventures.

From the east coast of Arran, they could look across to Bruce's family lands of Carrick. Ayrshire is divided into three sections. From north to south they are: Cunninghame, which stretches to the River Irvine; then Kyle down to the River Doon; and Carrick south of that. Bruce's mother was the Countess of Carrick, and he was most likely born at Carrick's main stronghold, Turnberry Castle, the remains of which stand round the lighthouse of the same name. King Edward had taken Turnberry and given it to Henry Percy, one of his leading magnates, and Percy lorded it there with 300 men.

Bruce decided to make a start on recovering mainland Scotland by capturing Turnberry. Taking his ancestral home would send out a strong signal that there was another force to be reckoned with in Scotland.

Bruce had a man from Carrick with him on Arran, Cuthbert by name, and he charged him with an errand. Cuthbert was to travel to Carrick by stealth and find out as much as he could about the English dispositions, and how the local people would feel about rising in the national cause. If he felt that the possibilities were ripe for a landing, he should light a fire near Turnberry point, and Bruce would set sail.

Bruce also explained to James that he had left two of his brothers with some Irish chieftains and a large body of men in Kintyre, and that they would make a landing further south in Galloway, so that it would become a two-pronged attack.

Several nights later a fire was seen in the darkness at a spot that looked near to Turnberry. Bruce's men, seeing this, quickly launched their galleys, and rowed with all their might, heading for the distant flickering flame. They found Cuthbert on the beach, somewhat distressed. He explained to Bruce that he found the land was overrun by Englishmen, and that the people were sorely abused, and suffered badly at their hands. They were not ready to join Bruce, and so he had not lit the beacon fire as planned. But there had been an accidental fire, a fisherman's hut had caught ablaze, and Cuthbert, seeing this, had feared that it might be mistaken for the beacon he was meant to light, so had made his way to the beach.

Bruce was in a quandary. He asked his men what they felt was the best course of action. Sir Edward, Bruce's brother, said that he would rather take his chances fighting the English than have to row back across the firth to Arran. Cuthbert informed them that 200 of the English were quartered in the village, and the rest in the castle. Bruce saw the chance. They could assail those quartered in the village if they approached secretly.

They crept close, then when it was seen that they had not been detected, they launched a furious assault, kicking in the doors and slaying every one of their enemies that they could discover. James played his part.

The hideous slaughter and associated noise terrified Percy's men within the castle, and they barred the gate, unsure of how many were their attackers.

While there, a kinswoman of Bruce, Christina of Carrick, gave him the news regarding his womenfolk – how some had been put in cages. She told him of his brother Nigel's execution.

Worse were the reports that the landing in Galloway had met with complete and utter disaster. The men had been attacked when they landed at Loch Ryan, just north of Stranraer. His brothers Alexander and Thomas, an Irish sub-king Malcolm MacQuillan and Sir Reginald Crawfurd had been taken to Carlisle. There, on the orders of King Edward, they were hanged and beheaded. Thomas's head was attached to a pole above the keep of Carlisle Castle, and the others had theirs spiked above the three gates to the town. I have never been able to pass Carlisle Castle without glancing to the top of the keep and thinking of poor Thomas.

I often think of Bruce in his extremity at hearing all this news. How does a man deal with so much hurt? There must have been constant questioning of all he had done. His ambition and desire to free his country had led to the people he loved the most suffering so much. An ordinary mortal would have gone under, but Bruce was a king, and knew he had to play that part and not waver in his beliefs. He realised that chivalry must be discarded. There were 10 Englishmen for every Scot. To try and meet them face-to-face in open battle would mean annihilation, and Scotland would be no more. He would show them. He would become a guerrilla fighter, even though what that term really meant was unknown at the time. He would strike Englishmen wherever he could find them, use his wits as much as his strength and do all he could to fight back.

At his side stood James. He took the king's aims and motives on board at once and was ready to teach King Edward and England that Scotland would never go down while he had breath in his body. He asked Bruce if he could leave him at this point, taking only two men with him, and go to Douglas to strike at those southerners who had taken his heritage. Bruce let him, though he feared what fate would befall his young friend. He watched him trot off, not yet knowing, but soon to find out, that James would teach them all how to fight using every means at their disposal, and that striking fear into Englishmen would become his forte.

CHAPTER FOUR

Forging of character by combat

JAMES AND HIS two companions made their way secretly to Douglas-dale. It is not a wide valley, just a few hundred yards of boggy flatland on either side of the meandering Douglas Water, rising to rough grassy hills, several hundred feet high. Perfect for cattle or sheep to graze. There was some cultivation here and there, where the ground was not too soggy. The castle stood on its rocky little crag, surrounded by marsh, down near the Douglas Water. The castleton, or village of Douglas, was about a mile west, further upstream, clustered round the old church of St Bride. Here and there in the glen stood the local farmers' little scattered houses.

James kept away from the more populated area near the village, and trotted up to the house of one Thomas Dickson at Hazelside, another mile or two to the west. James recalled Dickson being a loyal friend of his father. He had helped William Douglas and Wallace capture the castle at Sanquhar and had acted as a messenger between them. When James explained who he was, Dickson was so delighted to see the lad he had once known return as a man to his homeland, he shed tears. He quickly sneaked James into the house where they could talk. A plan started to formulate. Dickson knelt and took an oath of loyalty to James. He then sent for men from Douglasdale whom he knew to be loyal to Scotland's cause.

One by one they appeared at Hazelside and they too took oaths of loyalty to the son of their late lord William. Dickson told them all that on Palm Sunday, which was only three days away, the castle garrison would attend a service at St Bride's, along with many of the locals. This would be the time to strike.

James attended the service dressed as a thresher, his flail in hand, and wearing an old threadbare mantle. But under that mantle he was well armed. The English soldiers appeared from the direction of the castle, each carrying a palm leaf. They walked with arrogance and were full of self-confidence. They felt the land was cowed, and the people knew who their masters were. The 30 or so of the garrison crowded into the chancel of the little church. The folk of Douglasdale started to crowd in behind them. Each had a weapon secreted on their person.

A plan had been put in place. When all seemed normal and the English were settled, James would shout his slogan, and the Scots would fall upon their enemies, hopefully taking them completely by surprise.

But before everyone was prepared, the cry went up, 'Douglas! Douglas!'

Barbour tells us that on hearing this cry, Thomas Dickson threw himself into the nearest Englishmen, and managed to cut down two or three of them, but he was run through and slain. This is somewhat at odds with the fact that Bruce granted Dickson the lands of Symington in Lanarkshire in gratitude for his services. It could of course have been that Bruce honoured a son, and that Barbour did have it right. Certainly the house where he and James plotted was given to the family in perpetuity. As said, it was called Hazelside, and a later house of that name still stands on the site, on one's right as one travels west along Douglasdale close to where a minor road branches off the A70 towards Crawfordjohn. Dickson's descendents still resided there in the 17th century.

James, seeing Dickson assailed, took up the cry of 'Douglas!' and, sword slashing, cut his way into his enemies. The locals, impressed by James's prowess, and following his example, fell upon the English in an onslaught that killed 20 and resulted in the other 10 being taken captive. James sent half a dozen Scots running for the castle, but when they got there, there was only a cook and a porter left in residence. James and the rest, following from the church, walked into the castle unopposed. They found that the cook already had a meal prepared for the garrison's return from the church, and so James had the doors closed and invited his people to join him in a celebratory feast.

When the meal was over, they helped themselves to everything that was portable.

Like armour, swords, and spears and bows,
And money, valuables, and clothes

Everything else was destroyed. All the victuals like wheat, flour meal and malt were borne down to the cellar and scattered on the floor. James had the prisoners brought down, and there he beheaded them. He had taken on board Bruce's tactic of no chivalric honour. The invader had to be cleansed from the country, and that is what he would now do. The English had waged total war on Scotland, and James returned like for like.

The barrels of wine were brought down and added to the bloody mess in the cellar, and then James fired the place. He had kept what salt there was within the castle, and this he put down the well. He killed some English horses, and added these to the well for good measure, to make the place as unwelcome as possible for any future would-be garrisons. He stood back and watched the castle blaze, before asking his folk to gather up their wounded and make themselves scarce.

The locals, using that irreverence for which Scots are famed, soon spread the word of what had happened there, calling the affair 'The Douglas Larder'.

James had no option but to burn his family home. The English hold on Scotland was too powerful, there were various strong garrisons nearby, at Lanark and Bothwell for instance, and Ayr was none too far to the west. If he had held the place, there would have been no hope of relief if he was besieged. Hard as it must have been, he had to burn his own property. This behaviour became Bruce's strategy. Bruce realised there were far more Englishmen than Scots, and that they could easily garrison and overrun Scotland. But if each castle when taken was destroyed, or at least made uninhabitable, then they would have no safe haven. Billeted in towns and villages, or sleeping in the open, they could be attacked at any time. This led to a later rhyme, called 'Good King Robert's Testament':

On foot should be all Scottish war,
By hill and moss themselves to rear,
Let wood for walls be bow and spear,
That enemies do them no harm,
In safe places go keep all store,
And burn the plainland them before,
Then they shall pass away in haste,
When they shall find the land in waste,
With wiles and wakings of the night,

And great noises made on height
Then they shall turn made great afraid,
As though they were chased by sword away.
This is the council and intent,
Of Good King Robert's Testament.

James himself is reputed to have said he would 'rather hear the lark sing than the mouse squeak' in reference to the above. Just as well! For service to Scotland in the face of a larger enemy was going to ensure that James spent much of the next few years in either the saddle or the field.

For the next few weeks he, with only a few companions, skulked in the hills round Douglas. He had sent spies out with instructions to gather information. From this point on, James always liked to be kept well informed, and spies were always one way that he could keep ahead of the enemy.

Meanwhile, Bruce was gathering adherents in the south west. He kept to the rough hill country of Galloway. Though the English scoured the countryside for him, he always seemed to manage to keep one step ahead. By now he had several hundred men in his train. On 11 February King Edward of England wrote to his commanders in Scotland expressing his amazement that Bruce had not been captured. In response, the English raided into Glen Trool and were caught in an ambush, which resulted in heavy losses. It had been more of a guerrilla attack than a set battle, in line with Bruce's policy, and it had been a success. Methven was being avenged. And no matter how small the victory, it was still a beacon to the people of Scotland. There was a new force emerging in the land, and Bruce was making people wonder if the English hold was perhaps not as strong as some would have them believe.

The fight took place on the flat ground near the head of the loch, and most maps place it there, using the crossed sword symbol to denote its whereabouts. To find the memorial to the battle, erected in 1929, take the road that runs up the west side of Loch Trool from the A714. From where this road peters out in a series of parking places, it is only a few yards on. The memorial comprises a large rectangular block giving the details, standing atop a cairn of boulders, on a knoll that has a panoramic view over loch and glen.

Bruce was now able to strike north; the English stranglehold round him was temporarily broken.

One of James's spies brought him news of a large body of English troops, said to number 1,000, advancing south through Cunningham towards Kyle in Ayrshire. At most James had only 60 men at his disposal, but he knew if he could find a spot where his lack of numbers would not be easily discerned, he might be able to cause no little damage to the enemy. He knew the English were to advance down what Barbour calls 'Makyrnock's Way'. This route crossed a ford, called in his narrative Edryford. This ford was among marsh, and to the south of it was a rise, a narrow place, and James knew this was the place to conceal what numbers he had.

The Scots lay in ambush all night, and next day when the sun was shining they caught glimpses of the sunlight catching on armour in the distance. Eventually the English van, or advance guard, came into view, a banner flying at the front. The rest of the body comprised men on foot, and they came marching in tight ranks behind.

As the van crossed the ford, James and his men rushed upon them, and forced many back into the water with the ferocity of their attack. Other Scots in the undergrowth, armed with bows, fired wide-barbed arrows into the front ranks of the English, causing great confusion. With no idea of the numbers before them, the English could not push forward across the ford, nor could they go left or right because of the marshy terrain. The only real option was back through their fellows, but the rear ranks were still pushing on, and eventually panic set in, and he among them who could flee, began to do so.

The leader of the English, Sir Philip Mowbray, urged his horse onward and cut his way through the Scots. One man tried to hold him, but his sword belt snapped, and the man was left with Mowbray's sword in his hand. We are told that Mowbray galloped off through Kilmarnock, Kilwinning and Ardrossan, then through Largs to Inverkip, where the castle was filled with Englishmen.

Meanwhile James discovered that his men had slain 60, the rest of his enemies now fleeing for Bothwell Castle. This castle still stands in magnificent ruin, on a rise above a bend of the River Clyde, in the town of the same name in Clydesdale.

This leaves us with the problem of identifying the place called Makyrnock's Way in Barbour's text. George Eyre-Todd's 1907 translation of Barbour's original text states:

> This locality has always been obscure. Possibly it should be 'Maich and Garnock Way'. These two streams, descending from Misty Law towards Kilbirnie Loch, traverse the ordinary route of the present day from Clydeside into Cunningham. If this be correct the ambush was probably set at the old ford crossing the Maich Water among the marshes by Kilbirnie Loch.

But if the above is to be regarded as correct, then I'm afraid it does not really fit with Barbour's claim that Mowbray fled by way of Kilmarnock and Kilwinning etc. as mentioned above. A glance at a map of the area will show that this would be an unusual route to take from this location.

Local tradition in the Kilmarnock area puts this fight on the River Irvine, and Edryford at a locale somewhere between Hurlford (this name originating from another ford over the river, the 'whirl-ford'; for a while it was known as the 'hurdle-ford' too. 'Whirl' and 'eddy' mean the same thing of course, and it could be this is the root of 'edry', the Edryford in Barbour's narrative) and where the A77 crosses the river a mile or so downstream.

Since James's time, Hurlford has acquired much new housing, and it is difficult to ascertain what the ground would have looked like 700 years ago. But at least this area fits with Mowbray's flight, although he would have had to re-cross the river further west to have headed back through Kilmarnock. As you walk downstream to where the modern A77 concrete flyover crosses the Irvine, there is some banking on the south shore that could be where the Scots attack was launched.

All in all a bit of a mystery, but what makes it especially interesting is that some detective work could actually solve this problem, and it does not seem to be completely unanswerable.

Bruce was delighted to hear of James's success; defeating such a large force of the enemy with only three-score determined men. The Scots found themselves as a people during the reign of King Robert the Bruce in a way that they never have since. Several times during Bruce's struggle a mere 50 or so defeated several hundred, due mostly to great leadership. Scots need great leadership to bring out the best in them, yet seldom in their history have they got it.

Around this time, Barbour tells us a little of James's involvement in another episode. A trysting place had been set with Bruce, and when James appeared with Sir Edward, Bruce's brother, they were told of an incident in which enemies had beset Bruce, but he had managed to cut himself free and escape. Bruce knew there were English troops in the area under the command of Aymer de Valence, the English governor of Scotland, but the whereabouts of their camp was a mystery. James was able to inform Bruce that he had seen the English camp while on the way to this meeting, and that he knew the Scots could sneak up on the English, as they seemed unprepared for action and were scattered in various billets.

The Scots, some 140 strong, found that around 200 of the enemy were in a local village. There was no holding back, and they stormed the houses, killing every Englishmen they encountered. They then disappeared into the dawn, leaving the few English survivors to run to the main camp, where news of the carnage spread great alarm. De Valence was helpless in the face of such hit and run tactics, no matter how large and well equipped an army he led.

At the start of May 1307 he discovered that Bruce, accompanied by James and some 600 fighting men, and probably as many again in the shape of camp followers, grooms and the like, were encamped at Galston in the Loudoun Valley in Ayrshire.

De Valence issued a challenge to Bruce to stop his skulking, and to take the field in battle formation and pitch his men against the English in a chivalric fashion. This shows the arrogance of the invaders. They had forced their way into another country, yet asked its new monarch to behave like a gentleman and fight them in the field, simply because they desired it!

Probably very much to de Valence's surprise, Bruce agreed to meet him on the field of battle, and the time and place were agreed: 10 May at Loudoun Hill.

Loudoun Hill is the best part of 1,000 feet high, and stands above the infant River Irvine, east of the town of Darvel. It is said to be the most defensive site in all southern Scotland, and looking at its cliff-girt heights, it is easy to believe this claim.

Not that Bruce intended to use it as a defensive site. He planned to fight a pitched battle beneath it, but still to use the ground as an ally. A big part of Bruce's genius was his use of the landscape of Scotland itself to make up for lack of numbers. James had adopted this principle at Edryford. It was to stand them in good stead again and again.

The name Loudoun Hill is, in itself, an interesting one. It is made up of the Danish word for 'hill', which is 'law', the Scots/Gaelic 'dun', which also means 'hill', and the English 'hill', so it is law-dun-hill, or 'hill, hill, hill'! It is visible for miles around. It is the remnant of the core of an ancient volcano, like Edinburgh and Stirling Castle rocks. It has borne various defences on its summit over the centuries, with Roman and Pictish earthworks once gracing it. Today, climbers are often seen on its rocks, as it is a handy practising ground for challenging pitches further north.

Bruce got to the low ground to the south of Loudoun Hill a few days early. He inspected the ground with the eye of a commander. If he could beat an English army on the field of battle, it would be a rallying cry for all Scotland.

He noted how the road from Darvel on to Strathaven ran under the flanks of the hill, on wide firm ground that started to narrow with bog encroaching on either side. He saw his chance. He set his men to digging three rows of ditches across that narrowing firm ground. A 'bowshot apart', Barbour tells us.

Ditches to stop heavy cavalry do not need to be as deep or wide as one might think. Laden with armour, heavy warhorses are incapable of jumping even a minor obstacle, and if that obstacle is camouflaged it can become a real problem. And even a shallow ditch can make a horse stumble and throw its rider, who, encased in armour, can be greatly injured in the fall.

On the morning of 10 May, Bruce marched his 600 men forward in two divisions. They set themselves up at the chosen spot, their spear points outstretched, bristling like a hedgehog. The 3,000 English appeared from the direction of Darvel, and when they saw the Scots lined up in front, they spurred their heavy horse into a trot. To them, it must have looked very uneven, and they would have thought victory was assured.

They hit the first of the ditches, and some disorder was visible. Some shouted warnings, some shouted commands, and the ditch was crossed and the cavalry regrouped. On to the second and third lines of ditches, and confusion started to reign. Not only that, the firm ground started to narrow, and so the outer ranks pushed in a little, and the once-firm line that was meant to ride right over the Scots spearmen started to buckle.

Momentum was lost, and the first of the English horses hit the Scots piecemeal, to be met with those out-thrust spear points.

There was the agonised crash of metal on metal, and the Scots held firm, staking any steed or man that came within range. There were the screams of the wounded or dying, the neighing and whinnying of frightened horses. Then the Scots pushed forward, and the English fell backwards, confusion evident. Panic spread panic, and many Englishmen, deciding the day was lost, started to peel off. The Scots, sensing victory, redoubled their efforts. As the charge eddied and flowed and broke, they knew the day was won.

James stood amidst his men, urging, urging. No doubt drawing his sword and plunging in to cut down stragglers.

Loudoun Hill was lost and won, and Bruce had his victory. As the enemy streamed away to the west, there must have been great jubilation in the ranks. The story would spread like wildfire over Scotland, and many more men were to flock to Bruce's banner.

Atop Loudoun Hill today, just under the trig point on the summit, there is an inset stone commemorating this victory. Patriotic locals put it in place in the 1980s. Under the eastern flank of the hill there is a modern sculpture to Wallace, who also fought and won there. It is an inspiring metal creation, an outline of Wallace, with the hill itself framed by his silhouette. It is below the road that runs up that side, but cannot be seen from the road itself. You need to park in the little car park and walk the few yards down to it.

To ascend the hill, it is best to take the little farm road that starts opposite the Loudoun Hill Inn, which stands on the A71. It runs round the back to the northern side, where the gradient is not so tough, but the slopes are still steep and will be slippy in the wet. There are great views out, especially to the west, to the Isle of Arran and, if it is really clear, to Kintyre and Jura beyond.

Three days after Loudoun Hill, Bruce, accompanied by James, routed a force commanded by the Earl of Gloucester, and chased them back to Ayr. It seems his star was now in the ascendancy.

CHAPTER FIVE

Castle Dangerous

WE CAN BE sure that if the English had begun to show any interest in re-garrisoning Douglas Castle, word would have been quickly brought to James.

Barbour, several times in his text, mentions that James had spies bringing him information and says this of no other character, implying that he had built up a reliable network.

Word came that the English had indeed sent workmen to Douglas, and rebuilding had commenced. The stonework would have survived the burning at the time of the 'Douglas Larder', but new floors would have had to be put in, and the building re-roofed. Couldn't have been much fun clearing out the mess in the basement though, and clearing the well would not have been much better.

The new troops were under the command of one Thirlwall. James, after his arrival at Douglas, must have asked the locals questions about Thirlwall's character, and Barbour tells us James pulled a few stunts to see how Thirlwall would react.

Thirlwall made forays out into the surrounding countryside if he thought there was some personal gain, and James decided to take advantage of this. He gathered up some of the locals. Enough, he felt, to deal with anything Thirlwall could throw at him. He based himself at Sandi-lands, some six miles downstream on the Douglas Water. Sandilands is only a short distance from the point where the Douglas flows into the River Clyde. There was a Sandilands railway station at one time, if you want to hunt for the location of James's camp, but the station and the line are long gone now, although they are still marked on older maps.

At dawn the next day, James sent a few men to the castle environs to round up any cattle that were in that vicinity. They then made off with them downstream towards Sandilands. Thirlwall, when informed, called his men to arms and strapped on his armour, although it was reported he was bare headed when he set off in pursuit.

The rustlers were well ahead by this time and the English followed them in no great order. As the pursuit went on they really began to string out. The rustlers passed James's position, and he held his hand till most of the English pursuit were also past, as he wanted to make sure their retreat to the castle was cut off. Then the Scots ran out, taking the English completely by surprise. They went into full attack and hit the enemy so hard that few got away.

Thirlwall was cut down and slain, perhaps by James, who knew that seeking out and slaying the leader was the best way to demoralise the rest of the enemy. He and his men then chased the survivors back in the direction of the castle. Some managed to get within the gates, but by this time the Scots had caught the rearmost, and were slaying all that they could. The English garrison, watching this in a panic, closed the gates, leaving a few of their fellows to their doom. James and his men had to content themselves by taking whatever they could from round the castle, and then made themselves scarce. The English may have had superiority in numbers, but they had no way to deal with this kind of attack, this kind of hit-and-run warfare.

James was to make them wonder what they were doing in this land. Especially in the vicinity of Douglas Castle. Many years later Sir Walter Scott would call this place 'Castle Dangerous', and James, a man determined to take back all that was rightfully his, ensured that this was a fitting description.

On 15 May, a Scot who was fighting on the English side sent a letter to his master, which has survived. We can imagine how the news of Glen Trool and Loudoun Hill spread through the people of Scotland, and the effect it had. This letter gives us an insight into that:

I hear that Bruce never had the goodwill of his followers or of the people generally so much with him as now. It appears that God is with him, for he has destroyed King Edward's power both among the English and Scots. The people believe that Bruce will carry all before him, exhorted by 'false preachers' from Bruce's army, men who have previously been charged before the justices for advocating war and have been released on bail, but are now behaving worse than ever. I fully believe, as I have heard from Reginald Cheyne... that if Bruce can get away in this direction or towards the parts of Ross he will find the people all ready at his will more entirely than ever, unless King Edward can send more troops; for there are many people living loyally in his peace so long as the English are in power. May it please God to prolong King Edward's life, for men say openly that when he is gone the victory will go to Bruce. For these preachers have told the people that they have found a prophecy of Merlin, that after the death of 'le Roy Coveytous' [Edward] the people of Scotland and the Welsh shall band together and have full lordship and live in peace together till the end of the world.

From May till September Bruce concentrated on consolidating his position in Scotland's south west. He was ruthless, putting down any resistance to his rule from either reluctant Scots or English, with James his constant companion. He fought a hard campaign against his foes in Galloway.

King Edward of England put various laws in place to try and break the will of the Scots. They were told that anyone who took the patriotic side would be burned, or dragged by horses then hanged. Walter, the compiler of the English *Guisborough Chronicle*, tells us that the Scots then flocked to Bruce, because they would rather die fighting by his side than be killed by English law being imposed on Scotland.

Then, on 7 July 1307, English Edward died while trying to lead a final invasion into Scotland. He had based himself at Lanercost Priory, some 10 miles east of Carlisle, living in the guesthouse he had built for himself. He was there for the last few months of his life to try and direct the operations against Scotland. You can still visit the priory and the guesthouse; both are still in use. The guesthouse is a private building and can only be viewed from the outside, but the priory is open to visitors. They stand near Brampton.

Word had reached King Edward of Bruce's victory at Glen Trool, and although ill and 69 years of age, he decided to lead another army over the Border in person, and to destroy Bruce once and for all. He was being carried on a litter, but when he reached Carlisle he declared himself fit, donated his litter to Carlisle Cathedral, and marched his troops towards the Solway Firth, where he intended to invade by crossing the Solway sands at low tide. There, at Burgh by Sands, some six or seven miles north of Carlisle, he took his final breath, looking across the water at Scotland, but not standing on its soil. His huge army surrounded him, standing motionless and silent, waiting for news of how the king fared. A monument marks the spot where he died.

This monument, in the shape of a pillar surrounded by an iron fence, stands a little to the north of Burgh by Sands (pronounced 'Bruff by Sands') on the Burgh Marsh, and is reachable by a footpath from the village. It was erected in 1685 by Henry, Duke of Norfolk, and was restored in 1803 by the Earl of Lonsdale.

The chronicler Froissart, writing over 100 years later, stated that when King Edward knew his end was near, he told his son, the soon-to-be King Edward II of England, that he wanted his body boiled in a large cauldron till the flesh fell away from the bones. The flesh was to be buried, and his skeleton preserved. And each time the Scots rebelled (just like Edward – how can Scots be rebels to England?), this skeleton was to be borne before his army till the last Scot was crushed underfoot. He believed that 'as long as his bones were carried against the Scots, those Scots would never be victorious.' From what we know of Edward's character and his hatred of the Scots, this could well be true.

The *Guisborough Chronicle*, though, says that he was suffering from dysentery, and states that when Edward's servants lifted him from his bed on the morning of 7 July so that he could eat, he died in their arms.

An interesting book, *The Death of Kings* by Clifford Brewer, studies the causes of death of medieval and later monarchs of England using modern diagnoses. Brewer believes that Edward was suffering from cancer of the rectum.

Edward II was a different character altogether from his father, and he had Longshanks' body sent south to Westminster Abbey, where it still lies. Edward's tomb, of Purbeck marble, has the inscription 'Edwardus Primus Scottorum Malleus Pactum Serva' on its side. This is Latin for 'Edward the First, hammer of the Scots, keep faith.' Tradition states that Edward's body lay in St Michael's Church in Burgh by Sands for a few days till arrangements were made. This church is on the site of a Roman fort on Hadrian's Wall, and its stones were obviously purloined from the wall itself.

His entrails and brain were removed, purely because it was a long journey down to London in those days, and rotting would have set in long before his corpse reached its last resting place. These parts were taken to the abbey of Holm Cultram, which stands in the little village of Abbeytown, some 18 miles west south west of Carlisle. There is no marker to the fact that some of Edward was interred in the church, an eerie place, where I found the temperature to be much lower inside than out. Strangely, the father of Robert the Bruce was buried there, and his tombstone has survived. It stands upright, set in the wall of the porch.

Unfortunately, a fire seriously damaged the old abbey of Holm Cultram on 9 June 2006, but it is hoped that the money can be found to help restore this building to something like its former glory. Prince Henry, son of King David 1 of Scotland, founded Holm Cultram in 1150. Cistercian monks from Melrose Abbey settled it. So it has very Scottish roots.

So, King Edward, the bogeyman, the man who started this war of expansion against Scotland, was gone. The Scots must have breathed a huge sigh of relief when news of his demise arrived. They knew the son was not from the same mould as the father, preferring court life and the company of his 'favourites'. They knew that things would change, that the English impetus would not be so great – but this did not change the fact that there were 10 Englishmen for every Scot, and that England would continue its quest to annex Scotland.

Bruce knew that he had to go towards the north east of Scotland to show his power there. That part of the country round Buchan was very anti-Bruce, having much in the way of blood ties with the murdered Comyn. It was just unfortunate that many of Bruce's enemies showed their displeasure by siding with the English. There has always been that element in Scotland, folk who do not put Scotland first, and display that by siding with England.

That element was there 700 years ago and it exists today. And just as I and others are patriots where our country is concerned, we had James and his like all those centuries ago. They set a hard but good example for Scotland. And it is a shame that the other side of the coin still displays itself, and the fight that James and his like fought still needs to be fought today.

Come September 1307, Bruce crossed the 'Mounth', the area of high ground that comprises the eastern Grampian Mountains, to make sure the people there knew who was now monarch in Scotland. With

Edward dead, this was the time for Bruce to consolidate his position in the north east of his own country.

James was left behind in southern Scotland to wreak havoc against the occupying English there. He had obviously grown hugely in stature in the eyes of not only Bruce, but of the Scots troops in general. He was still only 21, but was showing great leadership qualities, and it seems his prowess in battle was not doubted by any. He was becoming a trusted and able commander.

We have little snippets of his movements. We hear of him in the forest around Paisley in September. He had managed to break the English hold in the area round Douglasdale, although the castle was still held against him.

After the slaying of Thirwall, the new governor was Sir John of Webton. James would soon deal with him, but in the interim, he made raids into the Selkirk area. Selkirk stood in the heart of its own forest, which was in itself an extension of the great Ettrick Forest, which covered much of the area around the upper Tweed and Teviot rivers. The English could only really hold on to the forest superficially as they could easily be assailed in its depths and fastnesses, and so James was determined to make it his own, and he would strike from it without warning.

He also cleared the English from Jed Forest, the heavily wooded area surrounding Jedburgh, near the Border. All the forested areas of the middle part of the Borderland of Scotland, whether Selkirk, Ettrick or Jed Forest, were actually known purely and simply as 'the Forest' to Scots at that time.

The Forest survives in part, but much depleted from what it was 700 years ago. James at that time was unable to threaten the great fortresses of Scotland in English hands, so he would take the Forest and make it a huge no-go area.

It did not matter how many troops the English had in garrisons surrounding the Forest, they were helpless to deal with the guerrilla tactics James employed. If they went out foraging for food, James could appear from the forest depths, cut them to ribbons, and disappear again into its fastnesses.

But the time came when he felt secure enough to return to Douglas and deal with Webton. He was a cautious man when it came to problems in warfare. James, like Bruce, would never risk a single Scot's life if he could think of a way to prevent it. His personal bravery had never been in doubt, but he would always look for an alternative to waging a pitched battle. His tactics were exactly what Scotland needed in this instance. He knew this, and would use his wits to do all he could in Scotland's defence, without risk to life and limb.

James used a variant of the scheme he had employed successfully against Thirwall. He had 14 of his men load sacks of hay on horses and take them by the castle, in full view of those on the battlements. It was market day in Lanark, some 12 miles away to the north east, and the English thought that these Scots were headed there. It would be easy pickings to overtake the Scots and take whatever they had for market. James and the rest of his band hid nearby, waiting to see if the English would take the bait.

And take the bait they did. Barbour tells us that Webton was:

A bold young man, of cruel fame,
But handsome and licentious,
And as he was so amorous,
More ready was he to go out

James waited till Webton and his men had passed his hiding place, and their retreat to the castle was cut off. At this, the men leading the hay-sack-laden horses threw the loads from the horses' backs and cast off their own simple peasants' robes to reveal their weapons beneath. They then mounted the horses, and with a shout turned to face the oncoming enemy. Great was the astonishment among the English when these peasants, who had looked like easy prey, turned out to be a force that meant business.

They were even more astonished when they looked back toward the castle and saw James and the rest of his band emerging from hiding. Panic set in and the English wavered, not knowing which way to turn. Then the Scots were upon them, and Barbour tells us that none escaped with their lives. Sir John Webton was cut down.

James immediately steered the Scots round and back towards the castle. The castle fell, but James, unlike in a previous escapade, allowed the garrison, men and boys, to make their way back to England unharmed.

The Scots rifled through the contents of the castle. In the coffer belonging to Webton, a letter was found. It was from a lady. She was obviously Webton's sweetheart, and she requested that he, to prove his love, should captain the castle of Douglas, which 'was so hard and perilous to hold', for a year. This was to prove that he was worthy of her admiration, and deserving of his expected reward.

But the lady had made a grave error in setting him such a task. James was not one to suffer foreign occupation of his patrimony, and Webton lost his life. To ensure that this constant re-garrisoning of the castle would not happen again, James had his men set themselves to its demolition, and breaches were made in the stone walling. The surrounding houses were pulled down too, ensuring that there was no place for the enemy to shelter.

James, accompanied by all the Douglas men who would join him in pursuit of the liberation of their country, made his way back to the Forest, where he continued to attack the invader, and his legend grew in the process.

CHAPTER SIX

In the service of the king

BRUCE CONSOLIDATED HIS POSITION in the north, although he took ill outside Huntly. Barbour tells us that it was due to his constant living of a life on the edge, full of alarums and surprises, and having to sleep in the open. The fact that all his brothers bar one had been tortured and killed by the English must have preyed on him, never mind the fate of his womenfolk, in their cold cages and the like. It was good that Bruce was made of the stern stuff of kings, but even he had his limits, and he could succumb to illness.

He did recover of course, and led his men to resounding victories in the north east. He then wasted much of the land of his enemies, in a campaign that became known to history as the 'Hership of Buchan'.

James seemed to be made of steel, though he was of course a dozen years younger than his king. He was able to absorb all the rough living that the service of his country required.

Bruce's surviving brother, Sir Edward, fought to consolidate Galloway, in the south west. He was a brilliant cavalry commander, but lacked the king's judgement, and he could be rash and impetuous at times, but he too was made of brave stuff. He differed greatly from James in attitude. He judged everything by his honour, but that honour could put his men at risk, as he would take on serious odds to prove a point. James would never take other than a very calculated risk. In this he mirrored his king. Bruce too would never risk a pitched battle unless he was sure that he was not putting any of his subjects in unnecessary danger.

James concentrated on his own sphere of operations, with royal consent of course. He had control of Douglasdale, of much of the Forest, and was making inroads into Lothian and the eastern Borders.

During his forays, James would appear at various places unannounced. On one occasion, as night was falling, he decided he and his men should take quarters in a building at Happrew. Happrew is near Peebles, in the vicinity of the Lyne Water. Wallace, accompanied by Simon Fraser, had one of his last fights against the English in its vicinity. The name survives in the farms of Easter and Wester Happrew today.

As James and his men approached in the failing light, voices were heard from within the building. James crept close and listened. He recognised one or two voices, and the subject matter discussed gave him clues to other identities. At his signal, his men drew their weapons and surrounded the place. Those inside were alerted, and grabbed their weapons, but though they tried to put up a brave defence, they were soon overpowered by James's hardened and fearless band.

One of those who fell into James's hands turned out to be quite a catch. It was Thomas Randolph, Bruce's nephew, who had been captured by the English at Methven. He had agreed to fight for the English from that point on. This was not an unusual occurrence in those days. When captured, combatants would agree to fight for the opposition, as a form of ransom, or simply because they wanted to be on the stronger side!

Many fought for the riches that warfare could bring, and saw no shame in this practice. But the Scots were fighting for their very existence in this war, and James knew where his patriotic duty lay, no matter how long the odds. He would never have taken the road that Randolph took, although one unreliable account from this era says that he did try to come to England's peace. As this is said to have happened when James's career was very much on the up and up, it is probable that it is nothing more than hearsay.

James took Randolph to Bruce himself, and the king was very pleased to see his nephew brought back into the fold. But Randolph did not see it that way. His English 'masters' had corrupted his mind where Bruce was concerned. They had pointed out to him that Bruce was a mere upstart, not a 'real' king like that of England. This was a man who skulked in the hills of Scotland, and did not fight in the chivalric manner. The English had even given Bruce a nickname. They called him King Hob, which in modern parlance basically means 'King Bobby'.

The fact that Bruce was fighting for the freedom of a nation did not come into it. There could be no rules where the very survival of Scotland was concerned, and Bruce knew this. The English greatly outnumbered the Scots, and to fight them in the chivalric manner would mean that Scotland would go under. Bruce would do everything in his power to make sure that this did not happen. Obviously James knew this, and followed this example. He was a true Scot, a true patriot, and would give all, life itself, to ensure his country's survival.

But he had wits and used them to the best of his ability.

Bruce must have listened with jaw set and eyes narrowed to the tirade regarding his character that emanated from his nephew. He had the power to order his death, but this was his own flesh and blood. He decided to take Randolph with him on his campaigns. He would be kept under close guard, but allowed to see the realities of the war that Bruce was waging. Bruce hoped that Randolph would 'grow up', so to speak, and see that it was his own nation, his own soil that was being fought for. He hoped that a hard lesson would touch Randolph's Scottish blood, rousing his own patriotism.

It did come to pass. Randolph eventually acceded that Bruce was right and fell into line. Bruce granted him the Earldom of Moray (pronounced 'Murray'). Randolph was to prove to be a stalwart in the Scottish cause. He resembled Bruce in many ways. Bruce's patriotism wavered somewhat in his early days, and it seems his nephew had followed him down the same road. But, again like his uncle, once the penny had dropped, he was a rock in the service of his country. James had returned him to the fold, and he and Randolph were to share many adventures. In James and Randolph, Bruce had two of the greatest captains that Scotland was ever to produce. Different personalities, but they worked brilliantly both alone and together to ensure the continued fight for Scotland's freedom.

Bruce had to wage a continued war, not only against the English, but also against those Scots who did not recognise his kingship. One of these was John of Lorne, who had instigated the attack on Bruce's company at Dail Righ. Bruce decided the time was right to march against John of Lorne's lands. We are not sure of the exact date, but it was probably in August 1308.

James accompanied his king on this foray into the western Highlands. It was known that John of Lorne based himself at Dunstaffnage Castle. This castle, once the home of Scotland's talisman, the Stone of Destiny, stands on the southern shore at the entrance to Loch Etive, a sea loch. Its ancient walls, following the contours of the rock on which it stands, are still complete today.

The chances are that the royal army came round the head of Loch

Awe, following the line of the modern A85 road. As the guides pointed out the v-shaped gap disappearing into the distance to the left of Ben Cruachan – the Pass of Brander – Bruce must have baulked a little. It was such an obvious defensive spot. Bruce was a tactician *par excellence*, and the constrictions of that pass were obvious even at that distance. He knew they had to force their way through the pass, and he also knew that it was where John of Lorne would destroy him if he could.

Loch Awe formed a boundary stretching to the south, cutting some 20 miles through rough Highland terrain. Ben Cruachan, rising from sea level to 1,126 metres, along with its outliers, formed an unbroken chain to the north. John of Lorne knew Bruce had to come this way, and he must have been reasonably confident that the pass could not be forced against determined defenders.

Barbour tells us that John of Lorne had a force of some 2,000 men to hold the pass. It would not be a case of just blocking the way through. The hillside plunges steeply from the summit of Cruachan, down to the deep, narrow arm of Loch Awe, which eventually pours out of the other end of the pass as the River Awe. Men posted above would be able to pry loose rocks, which would fall with crashing ruin on the men below. A determined few could easily hold Brander against many times their number.

Bruce knew that this was like the attack he had mounted at Glen Trool in reverse, and on a grander scale. He had easily destroyed his enemies in that encounter, and so had to think of a ruse to counteract the advantage that John of Lorne had.

On a decent morning in Scotland, the mist tends to linger on the hills, and then to rise as the sun heats the air. Bruce could use this to his advantage. He called for James, knowing he was just the man to carry out the job he had in mind. He told James that first thing the next morning, he was to take a force of lightly-armed men, most with bows, up the flanks of Cruachan. They were to make their way along the heights till they were above the pass. From there they would make their descent under cover of the mist, till they were within bowshot of John of Lorne's men.

Bruce, meanwhile, would march his main force along the pass as if trying to force the way. He would keep the attention of Lorne's forces focused on him, and hopefully James would be able to attack from above in complete surprise.

Next morning Bruce marched forward towards the jaws of Brander. Today the road and rail line hug the shore, right on the water's edge. They follow the path that Bruce took. The slopes of Cruachan soar upwards from the trackside. It must have been daunting entering the trap, the way so narrow that the horses were strung out in single file.

John of Lorne was a lame man, and so was not of the mould of a warrior. He was spotted out in the loch in a galley, where he could watch the drama unfold. His men, on the hillside, knew that he was watching their conduct, and would fight with all their ability.

Bruce took his force forward into the confines of the pass. He just had to go forward, knowing that the enemy would wait till his men were well and truly in the line of fire before unleashing their attack. He must have trusted James and his abilities implicitly, knowing that his involvement would be crucial to his men's survival.

John of Lorne's men suddenly attacked, rolling boulders down to cause mayhem among Bruce's long drawn out column. Their intention was obviously to break Bruce's men's spirit, and any cohesion that they might be able to put together. Then John of Lorne's men would draw their weapons and, using their uphill advantage, would charge down in superior numbers and finish the royal army off.

But Bruce had some nimble men ready, and at the first onset, he sent them scrambling up the hillside to get to grips with Lorne's men.

At the same time, in a position above, James and his men, previously hidden from the enemy by the now rising mist, jumped from their positions, and unleashed volleys of arrows down into the backs of Bruce's attackers. Lorne's men, realising that they were assailed from two sides, tried to put up a manful defence, but at their wavering the party below doubled their efforts. James then drew his sword, and at his signal the rest of the party dropped their bows and did likewise. Shouting his slogan, 'Douglas! Douglas!', he ran down to break the last resistance, his men nothing loath, running down headlong at his back.

Lorne's men fought bravely, but they were no fools and realised that there was no advantage in holding the position they were in. They began to break, eventually to run, and they fled westwards to the far end of the pass. Where the River Awe tumbled out in its rapid course down towards salt water at Loch Etive, the path crossed a bridge. They knew this and thought that they could regroup there and hold Bruce back.

When they reached the bridge, they tried to destroy it, thereby stalling Bruce. They would then have time to regroup and put up a more concerted defence. But the foremost of Bruce's men saw what was afoot, and ran forward, scattering the men trying to dismantle the structure.

When Bruce's army crossed the bridge, John of Lorne's men knew that the campaign was lost, and they scattered, leaving their dead and dying behind them. Lorne himself, seeing the defeat from the deck of his ship, turned and sailed to safety. Bruce and James were able to move forward to the shores of Loch Etive, where they captured Dunstaffnage Castle, Lorne's principal stronghold.

Following the road towards the pass through Lochawe village today, there is a beautiful, comparatively modern church by the name of St Conan's on one's left. It is worth visiting to gaze at its mock-gothic magnificence. But the visitor should not miss the giant effigy of Robert the Bruce that lies in repose within, especially as that effigy contains a piece of bone brought here from Bruce's tomb in Dunfermline Abbey to commemorate the fight that took place in this vicinity.

After consolidating his position in Argyll, Bruce held a council at Ardchattan Priory on the north shore of Loch Etive. He must have used the ferry that existed then to cross the loch. James would have been present, and in a dominant position. His rise to power had been meteoric, but completely justified by his actions and ability.

John of Lorne went to Edward II of England, looking for patronage there. His father, Alexander, submitted to Bruce and must have been present at Ardchattan, but he was soon to revert to form and rejoin English Edward.

The ruins of Ardchattan Priory still stand. Once the Connel Bridge at the narrows at the mouth of Loch Etive is crossed northbound, the road designation being the A828, the priory is signposted to the right, and it stands a few miles east along the loch's northern shore.

There have been gardens surrounding the priory since the 1300s, and the modern version is impressive. The more recent version of the priory is a private dwelling, but the ruins of the original standing round about it are open to visitors. There are really only rudimentary remains, but the grave slabs on show are well worth seeing, some bearing effigies of armed Hebridean-style warriors.

James accompanied Bruce on his journey south. They visited Inchmaholm at the end of September. Inchmaholm is an island in the Lake of Menteith, on which stands an impressive ruined priory. It can be visited, a boat plying the way to it from the shore at the Port of Menteith. The priory has some medieval tombs, including that of the betrayer of Wallace, and also has Mary, Queen of Scots associations.

In the first half of October 1308, Bruce and James were at Dunkeld, where once stood a castle, now long gone. The name 'Castle Close' gives an indication of its site. But it is possible they lodged in the cathedral, which still stands, partly ruined, partly restored, on the bank of the River Tay. They then made their way to Perth. Bruce's brother Sir Edward was consolidating the south west. Bruce had already brought the north east under his sway. But many of the major castles were still in English hands. These would have to be dealt with next.

CHAPTER SEVEN

Scotland's castles regained

KING ROBERT THE BRUCE in his wisdom knew that the English hold on Scotland depended on its castles and fortresses. The Scots were heavily outnumbered in terms of relative population, but it was not just about superiority in numbers, wealth and arms. To dominate the country, the English needed strong walls to feel secure behind and to garrison – somewhere to sleep unassailed. They could not dominate Scotland without this. Where would they sleep? In the woods and forests? These were places where the Scots could attack them at will. This simple truth became the staple of the next few years of Bruce's campaign. Very few stone castles survive in Scotland from before Bruce's time. Every one that he took, he destroyed or made undefendable. And more than that: he did it all bit by bit so that there was no major action that infuriated the English enough to make them mount another major invasion, nothing that did not make them think that if they focused themselves they could easily quash any Scottish resistance mounted against them.

Ordinary Scots took their king's lead. The English had a strong garrison in the Peel of Linlithgow, which was proving to be a thorn in the side of the locals with its continued deprivations. A local, Binnie by name, conjured up a plan. The English were used to having hay delivered by cart, so Binnie, aided by many friends, rolled a hay cart through the gateway and jammed it there so that the portcullis could not be lowered, whereupon his companions came out from under the hay, and others ran from the cover of nearby buildings. The porter was cut down and the building was taken back by its rightful owners. A grateful Bruce granted Binnie land for his endeavours, and this grant survives in the names of a local farm, West Binny, of Binny House, and of a local prominent hill, Binny Crag, near Uphall, which is worth scaling for the view and the sheer drop at one side.

Bruce made sure that the Peel was dismantled enough to make it untenable for the invader. The palace of Linlithgow, which stands on the site today, is of later construction than the early 1300s, but there is stonework on the exterior at its eastern side that was part of the original from Bruce's day.

Scots, instilling themselves with pride, came forward to help Bruce wherever they could. Phillip, the 'Forester of Plater', aided Bruce in the capture of Forfar Castle. The site of Forfar Castle still exists, a mound hidden behind shops in the town centre.

As is usual in times of war, advances were made in technology. In James's personal following was a man by the name of Sim of the Leadhouse. Leadhouse is the name of an old estate in the vicinity of Crossford in the Clydesdale, part of the parish of Lesmahagow.

Lesmahagow has the little-known scant ruins of a Tironensian priory beside its later church. The priory was built in 1144, so would have been familiar to James, Lesmahagow being the parish to the north of Douglas. There is an interesting little story attached to this priory. It was burned in 1335 by invading English under the command of John, Earl of Cornwall, brother of Edward III of England. When John later met with his brother the king at Perth, Edward slew him. According to the chronicler Wyntoun, this was because:

The vengeance fane perfay
Of the burning of that abbey.

It is thought from his name, and the fact that lead was once mined in this vicinity, that Sim of the Leadhouse might have been a lead miner, which might partly explain his ingenuity. Sim came to James with an invention he had made. It was a rope ladder, perfect for the needs of the Scots military machine at that time. Rope ladders, of course, can be rolled up and carried behind one's saddle on horseback, which was a bonus in those days of limited transport. Sim had crafted a large hook, with two rings attached. On the bottom ring the ropes for the ladder with its wooden slats would be tied. The other ring stuck out the back part at a right angle. The Scots in war carried long spears, which they used in their massed schiltrom, or hedgehog formations. This ring could be looped over a spear point, and the whole ladder assembly silently raised and the hook put into place over the parapet wall of a castle. As soon as the weight of the climber went on the first rung, it would cause the hook to grip even more securely on the stonework.

James was delighted with this gadget, and informed Bruce of its uses. The Scots began to employ such rope ladders right away, and under cover of darkness they would climb up and over the walls of English-held castles before the garrisons knew what was happening. Castle after castle fell, and the English really had no idea why so many fortresses were being lost. Eventually some Scots under James's command were disturbed while besieging Berwick and had to abandon a couple of their ladders. They were displayed in the town, and were spotted by the compiler of the *Lanercost Chronicle*, who described them in detail, noting that they were a 'wondrous construction'. Quite extraordinary that what seems such a simple invention to us today, was seen then as a huge leap forward in military technology. They may have been simple, but they worked brilliantly. The Scots did not have the wealth or the manpower to assail English-held fortresses with the great siege engines of that period, but Sim's rope ladders proved to be incredibly efficient and the need for long, drawn-out sieges and the loss of life they could entail were negated.

Bruce himself used this invention in his taking of the walled city of Perth in the winter of 1312–13. He had laid siege to the well-defended city during the tail end of 1312. For six weeks he kept up a fruitless assault, then packed up his goods and men and marched away, seemingly in disgust. But Bruce had had the town moat examined, and discovered a place where the water was not deep enough to stop determined men from crossing. He returned on the night of 7 January 1313, and under cover of darkness his men made ready to cross the moat with their rolled-up ladders. There was a French knight in Bruce's following, and he reported his astonishment when Bruce stripped naked and dropped into the icy water with the rest of his men. The water reached their throats, and it must have been bitingly cold in a Scottish January. The French knight was even more amazed when he saw that Bruce was the second man to cross the wall, his dirk clenched between his teeth!

Perth fell with very little struggle, and I'm sure that stories of Bruce's leadership in such cases did not just stiffen the resolve of the Scots, but would have endeared their king in their hearts too. Bruce would not risk lives unnecessarily, but he knew when to set an example that would give his people hope.

Other strongholds fell. All taken by stratagems and ruses. The English would not have thought of this type of warfare as being very gentlemanly or sporting, but it was what Scotland needed to survive. Bruce's brother Edward captured Rutherglen Castle, and though it is long gone, the town's Castle Street marks its site. More and more castles fell, till the English held nothing north of the Tay. Then it was nothing north of the Forth.

Many in the south were falling too, with Bruce personally taking the surrender of Dumfries.

Unusually for those times, and more so in the light of Edward I of England's treatment of captured Scots, Bruce was magnanimous towards many of those captured, releasing them in many cases. Then he would make the captured strengths uninhabitable, if he did not raze them altogether.

It seems that many of the defenders were Scots in English pay, though. The *Lanercost Chronicle* states:

> In all this fighting the Scots were so divided that often a father was with the Scots and his son with the English, or one brother was with the Scots and another with the English, or even one individual was first on one side and then on the other. But all or most of those Scots who were with the English were with them insincerely or to save their lands in England; for their hearts if not their bodies were always with their own people.

The words of our great bard, Robert Burns, 'Bought and sold for English gold', ring true down many centuries of Scotland's story.

James was not just acting the soldier during this time, of course. He attended parliaments, helped to steer the ship of state, and no doubt was involved in many meetings with other magnates. And there would have been audiences with his king, where as friends they could discuss the way ahead for Scotland's welfare and freedom.

James, as a landowner in the south, seemed to feel responsible for the security of Scotland's Border. Roxburgh Castle, one of Scotland's mightiest and most important strengths, lay close to England and so was easily resupplied by the enemy. Taking it would be a major step forward. Standing on a narrow strip of land that lies just west of the joining of the rivers Tweed and Teviot, it was really a walled town and castle, built atop a large oval mound, the rivers acting as a strong defence. It would be a formidable task to even approach the place, never mind climb the very steep 100 feet or so of banking to the base of its defensive walls.

As the years passed, James used his brains more and more, thinking up original ways to further Scotland's cause. These ideas were designed to prevent bloodshed on the scale that might be required in frontal assaults. What could he come up with to try and take Roxburgh Castle as simply and efficiently as possible?

On the night of 19–20 February 1314, James, accompanied by some 60 chosen men, hid his horses and approached the castle. In the murky darkness the men covered themselves with black cloaks, and on hands and knees they crawled along in single file, pretending to be stray cattle. I'm sure some of James's men wondered what on earth they were doing, warriors crawling in the mud. But I believe that they trusted James implicitly and knew he had their best interests at heart.

Barbour tells us:

And one man that was on the wall,
Did these words to another call,
'This man intends to make good cheer'
(And named a farmer dwelling near)
'Since he has left his cattle out!'

The guards then turned and went on their way, and James and his 'herd' crept to the wall and raised a rope ladder over the parapet. This ladder made a sound as it caught its grip. Sim of the Leadhouse clambered up, but a guard had heard the noise on the still of the night and ran to investigate. He reached the ladder just as Sim reached the top, but luckily Sim had his dirk drawn, and even more luckily the watchman did not try to raise the alarm, but leant over to throw Sim down. Sim grasped him by the neck and stabbed upwards into his body. Then he pulled him over the wall, and the unfortunate watchman fell among the Scots below. Sim, as loudly as he dared, told those below that all was well and to climb up with all haste. As James and the rest pushed forward to wait their turn to climb, another sentry appeared. He spotted Sim and knew he was not one of his comrades. Luck was again on Sim's side, as this sentry too made no alarm, but rushed forward to try and deal with him, although he drew no weapon as he approached. Sim was well armed and soon finished the man off.

James and the rest scrambled up, no doubt back-slapping Sim for a job well done, and they all stealthily made their way to the tower. The garrison, under the command of a knight named Guillemin de Fennes from Bouglon in Gascony, was celebrating Shrove Tuesday. They were drinking and dancing, completely at ease. It was the eve of Lent, and the custom then was to make merry on that date. To their horror, the cry of 'Douglas! Douglas!' went up in their midst, and James and his men stormed in, killing some and capturing others. The garrison tried to make a defence, but it soon collapsed and they began to flee in terror for their lives.

De Fennes managed to flee the hall and locked himself with a few companions in a turret. James's men ran riot through the castle, some of the garrison actually throwing themselves off the walls to try and make their escape.

The next morning, de Fennes realised that the castle and everything within the walls of Roxburgh was in the hands of James's men, but he was a brave knight and did his utmost to hold his position. There were many good bowmen among the Scots, and they fired constantly at the turret, looking for the gaps in its defences, making life for the men within as uncomfortable as possible. De Fennes held out for another day, but one of the Scots' arrows found its mark and he was badly wounded in the face, so much so that he feared the wound would prove fatal.

He asked James for terms, saying he would yield the tower if he and his men would be allowed to go to England unharmed. James granted this request, and off they went towards the Border, but we are told that de Fennes' wound was deep and wide, and soon after passing into England he died.

James sent Sim of the Leadhouse to the king, to inform him that Roxburgh had been taken. Bruce was delighted, and rewarded Sim for his part in the endeavour. The king then sent his brother Edward south with a great company to dismantle and tumble down the walls of Roxburgh, making it uninhabitable to the forces of occupation.

The scant remains of Roxburgh Castle stand just to the south of the A699, a little south west of Kelso. The large mound standing between the Rivers Tweed and Teviot is unmissable, with its surrounding ditch still clearly visible, one or two fragments of walling projecting from the summit. Finding somewhere to park is not easy, but there is a little inshot at the western end of the site with enough room for a couple of cars or a few motorbikes, and footpaths spread out over the grassy banks. You can walk, appreciate the views over the rivers at either side, and wander the few fragments of walling. Although there is really nothing left to connect it to the days of James the Good, you can put the story into perspective. Nice view out from the top too, looking over towards the very impressive Floors Castle to the north, the seat of the Duke of Roxburgh, which is open to the public. And you may or may not be interested to know that Floors posed as Greystoke in a Tarzan film. You can spot the remains of Kelso Abbey projecting over the roofs of the town, just as the garrison would once have been able to do. I once spent a brilliant summer's day with my family, skiddling in the waters of the Teviot below the remains, and I hope if you visit the place you will have a day that is as memorable for you.

There is a village a few miles away called Roxburgh, but this is one of those instances where the name has moved, and though it is a nice place it has nothing to do with the original.

Thomas Randolph, Bruce's nephew, once a man who stood against the Scottish cause, now Earl of Moray, began to show that he had inherited some of his uncle's spirit. He heard of James's exploits at Roxburgh and assayed to find a way to capture Edinburgh Castle. It was one of the mightiest strengths in the country, standing seemingly unassailable on its rock, the core of a long-extinct volcano.

A healthy rivalry had started to develop between Randolph and James, a rivalry that would have each of these dashing young men trying to outdo the other in feats of arms and ingenuity. Although this next tale of derring-do is really about Randolph, it gives a good example of the interaction between James and himself, and how each tried to match the feats of the other. Bruce was lucky in his captains, and lucky in the bravado that they displayed. Randolph was equally lucky when he came across a man by the name of William Francis, whose father had once been a member of the garrison at Edinburgh Castle. Francis had a girlfriend in the town of Edinburgh, and had found a way to climb down the castle rock of an evening so that he could spend the night with her, and then climb back before dawn so that none knew of his absence. He told Randolph that he could lead a party of determined men up the rock face to a point where there was only a 12-foot-high stretch of walling where they could hook their rope ladders over the parapet. Randolph, nothing loath, started to put the plan into operation, and set the assault for the night of 14 March 1314, just a few weeks after James's taking of Roxburgh.

A diversion was created to take the attention of the garrison, in which a body of Scots assailed the castle's East Port, where the castle esplanade stands today. Meanwhile, Randolph, with a party of 30 hand-picked men, began to follow William Francis up the north west side of the rock.

It was a dark, murky night, and the climb was not easy. Barbour tells us:

> The crag was high and hideous;
> The climbing was right perilous,
> If any chanced to slip or fall,
> He would be dashed to pieces all.

Halfway up the rock face Randolph and his men reached a ledge where there was enough room for them all to rest for a few minutes. They heard the voices of a few guards above them on the parapet wall, and held their breaths. They all knew that if they were spotted, all the garrison had to do was cast down a few stones and the results would be catastrophic, there being nowhere to find cover on their exposed position. In those days though, the darkness, with no light pollution, would have lain over them like a cloak. If it had been an evening of moonlight, the guards might have spotted the slightest movement, but as already stated, Barbour, using eyewitnesses, said that the night was murky.

The guards above paused, and the men below pressed themselves into the rocks. One voice above called, 'Away, I see you clear!', and someone tossed down a stone. Randolph and his men must have thought they were doomed, but a few seconds passed and the guards' chatter continued and they carried on walking along the parapet. The besiegers realised that it had merely been a jape by one of the guards.

Although the rock face above their resting place was even more severe a climb than that below, they pushed on, their hands feeling for cracks, their feet looking for purchase, adrenalin pumping.

Reaching the wall, a ladder was put in place. William Francis was the first over, a knight named Sir Andrew Gray was second, and third was Randolph himself. Others came scrambling up at their backs.

Members of the garrison heard the clink of arms and the whispers of Randolph's men, and a cry of 'Treason! Treason!' was raised. Defenders came running, but Randolph's determined bunch ran to meet the challenge and they fell back in disarray. The Scots fought their way towards the front gate, to fall on those facing the diversion being mounted there. The gate was opened, and the larger force stormed in. There was a great slaughter, the Gascon commander in English pay, Sir Pierre Libaud, surrendering. Libaud agreed to enter Bruce's service, but it was not a long-lasting arrangement, as he was soon executed for treason.

Again, in accordance with Bruce's policy, Edinburgh Castle was rendered useless to the English.

The taking of castles was going very smoothly, but there was one stumbling point. Bruce had asked his brother, Edward, to supervise the siege of Stirling Castle. From Lent 1313 till almost midsummer that same year, Edward Bruce was encamped at Stirling, his men forming a cordon round the castle. Their aim was to stop supplies getting through, to eventually starve the invaders into submission.

Edward was a brilliant cavalry commander, with a huge amount of personal bravery, but he could be reckless, and did not seem to have his brother's or James's instinct to never take undue risks. He would take on impossible odds – and often prevailed, due to his and his men's bravery. But the possibility of many Scots losing their lives was always in the background where Edward was concerned.

There was some skirmishing involved in laying siege to a castle like Stirling, but it was not enough to prevent Edward Bruce from seeing his task as a chore. He felt he was kicking his heels. He felt he would be better leading raids than vegetating here.

Edward struck a deal with Sir Philip Mowbray, a Scot who was fighting for the English and was in command at Stirling Castle. Edward made a pact that unless an English army came to within three miles of Stirling to fight for the relief of the castle before midsummer's day 1314,

Mowbray would hand it over to the Scots. This arrangement suited Mowbray as it meant the castle's supplies could be rationed to ensure the garrison's survival no matter what. And I'm sure he was no fool and knew the consequences of Edward agreeing to such a pact.

Edward Bruce thought he was getting the better deal, of course. He knew that the castle would have to capitulate. He knew that Bruce's men had been taking castle after castle from English control with no real retaliation from down south, and he was now spared the rigours of camp life and a boring siege. He happily went back to report to his brother the king that Stirling Castle was as good as theirs, thinking that he would be praised.

But the Bruce listened to the story barely able to suppress his rage.

He knew that this was a direct challenge to the might of England, a call to arms no less. King Edward of England's bickering nobles would unite and fight as one to crush the upstart Scots once and for all. Bruce was right: the call went out, not just over England, but all across Europe, one summons travelling as far as Constantinople to release Giles d'Argentan, reckoned the third best knight in Christendom. He and others were asked to come and share the spoils from the final crushing of Scotland.

Letters went out to France, to Gascony, Flanders and Brittany. Troops were summoned from Wales and Ireland, Hainault and Germany. Even those Scots who cravenly supported England were summoned and gathered to fight.

In light of this threat, we can see the mettle of soldiers like James and Randolph. Although they had a good idea of what they would have to face in the summer of 1314, they still went ahead and took Roxburgh and Edinburgh respectively that spring.

Bruce rebuked his brother for his part in putting Scotland's future in jeopardy, while trying to keep all in control because division was the last thing that Scotland needed. Even if judgement was not his brother's strong point, he was still a good soldier and could play the captain.

They had a year to prepare. A year before the mightiest fighting machine in Christendom came over their borders, looking to wipe out the ancient kingdom of the Scots, aiming to consign the name 'Scot' to the chronicles and history books.

CHAPTER EIGHT

Bannockburn

BRUCE WAS ENTIRELY RIGHT, of course. England saw this policy of relief for Stirling Castle as a direct challenge. While England sent out summons to her heroes, Bruce would have gathered his captains, including James, and outlined his strategy to defeat this dire threat to Scotland's survival.

I'm sure that during the past seven years of struggle, James had identified many men that he knew he could trust. Men who would not only take orders, but convey them to others and stand firm in the face of adversity. Bruce had informed James that he would be leading a division of the Scottish army, and James knew that within that division he would need men to pass on his commands.

We know that in the early months of 1314, James continued to rid Scotland of the English. The taking of Roxburgh Castle testifies to that. But it also shows us that the Scots felt that it was worthwhile to oppose the enemy in any way possible, even with the threat of the forthcoming invasion hanging over them.

Bruce would have had his spies out, keeping him posted of any troop movements on the English side of the Border. In this day and age, I think we sometimes don't really consider how difficult it must have been to keep tabs on enemy troop movements. Armies could pass within miles of each other, neither knowing of the other's proximity. Bruce must have had swift-moving riders travelling back and forward through the Border country to keep him as well informed as possible. The last thing the Scots wanted was a full-scale invasion force spilling unannounced over the Border, or a feint to distract them from the main assault. Luckily, with Edward II of England sending out summons to his 'loyal' Scots subjects, word would have filtered back that foot soldiers were to gather on 10 June at Wark-on-Tweed, and cavalry at Berwick upon Tweed, further east.

By mid-May, Bruce had his army gather in the Torwood for training. James was there, of course, to train with his own division. They had to learn the new tactics Bruce had developed to counteract the threat posed by the English heavy cavalry.

The Scots just did not have the money, or for that matter the horse-flesh, to mount a division of heavy cavalry of their own. The horses used were like modern Clydesdales. They were bred for bulk, as they had to carry their own armour, as well as a knight wearing eight stone of chain mail and plate armour, topped off with weaponry. These medieval equivalents of tanks could easily ride right over foot soldiers, so how to deal with them?

Bruce was probably present at Wallace's battle of Falkirk in 1298, where the Scots had used long spears to counteract repeated cavalry charges. The spearmen were formed into formations known as 'schil-troms'. These were like hedgehogs, the spears jutting out at all angles, with anything up to a couple of thousand men comprising the unit. They could impale either horse or rider, whilst forming an impenetrable barrier that thwarted heavy cavalry. Falkirk had been lost due to the English longbows firing arrows like hail into the schiltroms, the spearmen having no defence against that form of warfare; but Bruce knew that heavy cavalry had not been able to break the schiltrom unassisted.

So he decided to develop the idea. Wallace's spearmen had been static – dug in, so to speak. Bruce was training his army of spearmen to move as one unit, still impenetrable, but mobile. Training was all-important. Each man had to know exactly what was expected of him, and had to trust his fellows explicitly.

James had his own schiltrom to train, spending the next few weeks going over and over and over the techniques Bruce had outlined. He had somewhere between 1,500 and 2,000 men in his unit, and there were three others equally as large. We forget the logistics involved in all this. These men were there for a month, and all had to be fed and sheltered so that they were kept ready for battle. They all had to be armed, too. This required many thousands of spears, so there must have been many artisans working to make all those heads and shafts, to create the hardened leather tunics and helmets for all the troops.

They were deep in the Torwood, and I'm sure guards were making patrols to watch for unwelcome prying eyes.

The Torwood at that time stretched from the River Carron west and north towards Stirling, and inland towards the Campsie Hills. It was traversed by an old Roman road running north towards Stirling and the River Forth. Bruce would expect the English to come that way, using the road to approach Stirling Castle.

The Torwood still exists, though it is a shadow of its former self, the thickest remnants clustered round the village of the same name, standing not too far from the M876 near Larbert. The Roman road is still marked on Ordnance Survey maps. It runs by Torwood Castle and on through the woodland, and then a farm road follows its course to within sight of Stirling Services on the M9, the services only a mile or two from the battle site.

As midsummer's day grew close, Bruce drew his troops back to the position he had chosen to await the arrival of the English main attack. This was on a raised mound of hard ground surrounded by more marshy terrain, to the north of the Bannock Burn. The National Trust for Scotland Bannockburn Visitor Centre stands in the vicinity today. A large stone with a socket in it, called the Borestone, stood nearby. Bruce had the lion rampant banner thrust into this socket, flapping valiantly in the breeze. The steps leading up to the memorial rotunda mark the site of the Borestone, and remnants of it are kept within the visitor centre.

The Scots were facing the Roman road where it emerged from the Torwood. If they turned almost 180 degrees, they would see Stirling Castle standing proud on its rock, a couple of miles away.

The Scottish army was arrayed in four divisions. Bruce's was closest to the Torwood, and like the others contained somewhere between 1,500 and 2,000 men. These were the men from his own estates in Annandale and Carrick, along with many Highlanders, lightly armed but fierce fighters. Next in line was his brother Edward's schiltrom, comprising the men of south west Scotland. Then it was James. His schiltrom was nominally under the command of Walter the Steward, his cousin, and son of the High Steward of Scotland. But as he was fairly young and did not have James's experience, James was in actual command. Nearest the village of St Ninians, with its prominent church, Thomas Randolph, Bruce's nephew, commanded the fourth schiltrom.

Other than the four divisions, Bruce had some 500 light cavalry under the command of Keith, the Marischal of Scotland. Bruce had seen the effect of the bowmen on Wallace's schiltroms at Falkirk 16 years before, and he had a special purpose for these light horse.

Muster rolls exist for the English army, and it seems there were over 20,000 foot soldiers, not including the Irish contingent. Educated guesses put the amount of cavalry that King Edward II had available at 3,000. Over and above this, there would have been camp followers, workmen, armourers, smiths, and we are told that the baggage train, if strung out, would stretch for 20 miles. Many had come north to share in the spoil of a whole country, as Edward II had come to destroy the Kingdom of Scotland once and for all.

It would seem that the ratio of manpower between the two armies was in the region of three to one. But over and above that, the English had by far the superior weaponry.

The one thing we have always to bear in mind is the example set by Bruce. One Scot's life put at risk was one too many. He had eaten away at the English occupation piecemeal, making calculated stealthy steps forward, and had never risked open battle when there were other means at his disposal. Bruce never set out to go into battle at Bannockburn. If he could have thwarted English ambitions by other means, he would certainly have done so, and this must be remembered when the events of June 1314 are examined.

So, although battle was not a foregone conclusion, his spearmen were trained, his schiltroms were under the command of some brilliant young captains, and everyone knew what was required of them if a battle was to come. There were many good fighting men still coming into camp on a daily basis, coming to answer the call of their country. But Bruce could not let these men, no matter how renowned their prowess, join the schiltroms untrained in the tactics he required. He asked them to go back behind the lines of the main array to join the rest of the camp followers on top of Gillies Hill (the name is Gaelic for the hill of the 'Young Men', and takes its name from the events of 1314). With all the cooks and armourers etc., this must have been quite a sizeable force.

Bruce's scouts would have been bringing in reports of the advance of the English invasion force. They had crossed the River Tweed, most likely on 17 June, and had advanced up the eastern side of Scotland, taking the route of an old Roman road over Soutra. Crossing there, they would then have dropped to the soft central belt. They took the line of the modern A68, with its many wind turbines, familiar landmarks to the motorist. I suppose among those driving this ancient through route today, there are very few who stop to imagine a vast medieval army coming this way, with the destruction of Scotland uppermost on its agenda. There are the ruins of an old hospice at Soutra too, signposted from the A68, which existed back in the days of the Wars of Independence.

This army halted briefly at Edinburgh on 19 June. We are told that it was urged on to reach Stirling by the deadline agreed to by Edward Bruce, and so there was little time for eating, and only short periods where sleep was allowed. The troops pushed on the 20 miles to Falkirk on 22 June, and there they were only 15 miles from the Scots.

23 June 1314

Bruce's scouts were reporting how close the English were. When the English left Falkirk on 23 June, Bruce sent James forward with Keith the Marischal to watch the English host cross the flatland between Falkirk and the Scots' position. James was a vastly experienced soldier by this time, and he was appalled at the numbers approaching Bannockburn. The summer sun must have been glinting off armour, with many hundreds of pennants, flags and banners fluttering in the breeze.

James and Keith the Marischal returned to Bruce's position, and privately told him about the seemingly unstoppable force covering the plain before them. Bruce told them that they must keep this news to themselves, and that they should spread the story that the English were advancing in disarray. This was partly true. There was dissent among the English elite, many of the great lords of that country arguing about their place in the coming battle, and taking offence that they did not have the status that they felt their position deserved.

Bruce had some of his forces out on the edge of the Torwood, digging potholes to break up the expected charge of English cavalry. He knew that there were only two routes the invader could take, either a straightforward one along the Roman road to the Scots' positions, or a drop down to the lower land nearer the River Forth and across the carse land there.

Something that should always be borne in mind when looking at the logistics of Bannockburn is the knowledge that the commanders had of the ground – and not just the Scottish commanders. Many in the English army had been there before, some as far back as Wallace's battle of

Stirling Bridge in 1297, 17 years earlier. When crossing from southern Scotland to northern, most folk crossed the River Forth at Stirling, and as the English had been constantly manning garrisons in the north, many of their ordinary men-at-arms, never mind their captains, would have been across there several times.

Bruce was a master of using the terrain to his advantage, and aimed to negate any knowledge that the English had, hence the digging of these rows of potholes before the Scots' positions. If the English charged, he wanted them to hit these holes, two or three ft deep, some containing wooden spikes and covered with brush to conceal them. These would break up any assault by horseback and make the English very unsure of their position.

The pits can still be discerned by aerial photography, stretching across the slightly raised stretch of ground running from Pirnhall Farm west towards the M9. Some of the wooden stakes that the pits contained are on show in the Stirling Smith Art Gallery and Museum.

The English were following the line of the old Roman road through the Torwood, passing right by Torwood Castle. When they reached the vicinity of West Plean Farm, they sent off two heavily-armed divisions of cavalry. One went right, down onto the carse land of the River Forth to head for Stirling Castle, its line making it a little too low for the main body of Scots to notice it from the Borestone area. The other division, going left, cut through what was left of the Torwood and made directly for the Scots. This section of the Roman road, where the English started to deploy, is still in use as a farm access road today, running right by West Plean Farm. So you can still take the route that the English did on the day.

Bruce was out with his men, helping to direct the operations digging the potholes, when this latter English division burst through the trees. One knight, Henry de Bohun, the nephew of the Earl of Hereford, spotted the circlet of gold on Bruce's brow glinting in the midsummer sun. He cried, 'It is the King of Scots, he is mine!' and charged forward to take on Bruce in single combat. Bruce was unprepared for such an eventuality, was on a small pony, a hobin, and carried only his battle-axe for weaponry.

What happened next took place within the sight of the Scots divisions over by the Borestone. Bruce did not hesitate. Turning his horse's head and galloping for safety was unthinkable. Bruce had to deal with de Bohun, knowing the eyes of his army were upon him. De Bohun couched his lance, and aimed straight for Bruce. The Scots must have held their breaths at this drama, and James must have feared for his monarch. Bruce drew his axe. He was a master of this murderous weapon. It could be wielded at different angles to hack, slash, cut or stun. Just when it looked like he was going to be impaled on the point of the lance, Bruce savagely pulled on the reins of his pony, rearing the beast up onto its back legs. In the memorable words of Barbour, 'Sir Henry missed the noble king!' As de Bohun passed him, Bruce stood on his stirrups and raised his axe. He used every ounce of strength in his sinewy arm to bring it crashing down on the knight's great helm. Bruce was a powerful man, well built and six feet tall, and had trained in warfare and weaponry his whole life. He hit de Bohun with such force that he cut down through the metal of his helmet, through his chain mail, through flesh and skull, all the way to his breast bone. De Bohun's horse carried on for a few steps, then the Englishman fell from its back in gory ruin. Bruce had hit the knight so hard that the wooden haft of his axe had shivered and splintered, shattering in his hand. He was left holding a foot or so of wood.

Bruce led by example. Sitting on a little pony, lightly armed, he must have looked puny in comparison to the armoured de Bohun on his charger, yet he prevailed. This was not lost on the Scots army watching from the Borestone. The King of Scots himself had struck the first blow against the mighty invader. The rest of the Scots with Bruce assailed and repulsed the English squadron, bolstered by the actions of their king. The invaders retired to lick their wounds.

Bruce trotted back over to the main body of his army. His captains were aghast, and berated him. 'You are the king!' they cried. 'You risked too much there. If you had fallen we would all have been lost, it was a foolish gamble.'

James would have been among this group, worried as to what might have befallen his friend, but proud of the ability he had displayed.

Bruce replied, 'You are right, I broke my good axe!' And he looked ruefully down at the splintered shaft of wood in his hand.

This story would have been passed back through the ranks of the army, of course, losing nothing in the telling. The task that lay ahead of these men was, for a while, pushed to the backs of their minds, as they spoke with relish about the exploits of their king.

On the far side of the M9 from the Borestone, on the line of the aforementioned potholes dug by the Scots, there is a farm by the name of Foot o' Green. Local legend states that this farm stands on the site of Bruce's encounter with de Bohun. The name is supposed to have come from Bruce's rearing up on his little pony, and pushing his feet into the soft ground as he crashed his axe down! Certainly the farm seems to be in the right location, and stranger things have happened!

As Bruce was standing with his captains, he either glanced up, or was alerted by the exclamations of those nearby. The other division of English heavy cavalry, that which had branched off to the right at West Plean and skirted the edge of the carse of the Forth, out of sight of the Scots, had come into view as it reached the village of St Ninians. Randolph's schiltrom was at the rear of the line, and overlooked St Ninians from its slightly raised position. Bruce spun and saw that Randolph was standing amid the group that had clustered round him as he returned with his broken axe. He had probably been transfixed by the events that had occurred over at Foot o' Green and lingered after the outcome, but Bruce was anything but pleased.

He pointed out the body of English knights to Randolph. Bruce told him that he had posted him by St Ninians to guard the way to the castle, and here he was over by the king and away from his men. He informed Randolph 'a rose had fallen from his chaplet'. (This was apparently quite a strong rebuke in those days!) Randolph, stung, ran back to his men, determined to make amends.

He reached his schiltrom, barking commands, and his men, as one, spears bristling, moved forward towards the English cavalry.

The horsed body of English was under the command of Sir Robert Clifford and Sir Henry Beaumont, both seasoned veterans. The English never really expected the Scots to give battle, and the object of their manoeuvring was probably to cut off the Scots' line of retreat. There was a certain logic to this of course, because Bruce was still not committed to battle, but the English were arrogant enough to believe that they had only to turn up to win the day.

They probably had something like 600 heavy cavalry under their command, a terrifying and formidable force, with the best of armour and weaponry. They spotted Randolph's schiltrom, and Beaumont cried, 'Let them come on! Give them room!'

Randolph's schiltrom comprised somewhere in the region of 1,500 spearmen, which on paper should have been no formidable obstacle to a large body of heavy cavalry.

Randolph's men dug in as the English spurred their horses forward and came on at the charge. The Scots stood tight, waiting for the horrific crashing impact to come, each man depending on his fellows to hold the line and show no weakness.

With a yell the Scots braced themselves; then there were screams and the crunch of breaking spears as the two sides came together in a thundering smash of flesh, bone and metal.

The Scots seemed to be engulfed in a tidal wave of English horses, and were hidden in the resulting cloud of dust. James was watching from his schiltrom, the next along in line. It looked like Randolph's men must surely begin to buckle and be overwhelmed by the might of the English attack. He could stand it no longer. His friend Randolph and his men were surely going to be slaughtered. James ran to Bruce and begged leave to bring his schiltrom to Randolph's aid. At least marching onto the field of battle would perhaps distract the English and split their forces. But Bruce knew the main body of the English was near, and dared not risk weakening his army any further in case a major assault came.

Eventually James could contain himself no longer and started to order his men forward, but when they reached the edge of the slope leading down to the fight a different picture began to emerge. He could see that there was a great mound of dead and dying men and horses building up round Randolph's men, and the English had taken to throwing their weapons, swords, axes and maces at the Scots in their frustration. James, with his characteristic chivalry, shouted the order to halt. It seemed that Randolph was achieving that which seemed impossible, and at the same time, Bruce's tactics were being proven as sound. James could not go forward and take some of the glory away from Randolph. His men had displayed great valour, and should take the kudos for all they had done. Randolph sensed the frustration of the English, and that the waves of attack were growing weaker. He gave the order to advance, and as one the schiltrom moved forward, rolling over the last vestiges of the assault, and the English began to break and retreat.

James watched as Randolph's men, gasping for air, removed their helmets, clouds of steam rising from them after their exertions. It was said afterwards that spears splintering under the weight of horseflesh had claimed more of them than had been killed by English steel.

As Randolph's schiltrom returned to its place in the main body of the battle army, the men were roundly cheered and applauded by their compatriots. All now knew that their enemies were not invincible, no matter the disparity in numbers and arms. James would have cheered with the rest, and I'm sure his and Randolph's eyes met and those two hardened soldiers nodded an understanding to each other.

The spot where Randolph held the charge is still marked today. On the grassland in front of the police offices at Randolphsfield (pretty self-explanatory name!), on the road leading from St Ninians to Stirling, there are two standing stones. These traditionally mark the site of the fight. You can stand there and turn your mind to 1314, to Randolph's men holding off the repeated charges, and the ground behind where James watched their victory.

Twice the Scots had discomfited their enemies, and the day was growing late. King Edward II of England must have had his captains reporting back, and the news they were carrying was not what he wanted to hear. He came forward himself, and stood atop Craigford, a rocky little crag that stands above the ford where the Roman road crossed the Bannock Burn. From there he looked across at the Scots' position. The slightly raised ground round the Borestone was stronger than a first glance would perhaps have suggested. There was much marshy ground, and then a climb uphill to the schiltrom of the King of Scots.

Craigford is on your right as you drive from the services on the M9 down towards the Bannock Burn and on to the Heritage Centre. Even today, as you look out from the site of the Borestone, there are still some reed beds remaining of the old Milton Bog, showing how defensive a position this once was.

King Edward decided that the Scots' position was too strong for a frontal assault, and it was too late in the day to take further action. So the English army needed to find a place to bivouac for the night. Somewhere with water for the horses, and an open space where they could not be easily assailed during the short midsummer nights.

A fateful decision was made. The English army would spend the night out on the low-lying carse of the River Forth. The army then swung to the east and followed the course of the Bannock Burn onto the low ground. From the Scots' position down onto the carse, the Bannock flows down through a deep, steep-sided gorge. The English followed the opposite bank from the Scots downstream, and spread out on to the carse. It was boggy there, with sluggish streams and pools. The English actually had to requisition doors and woodwork from local houses to create makeshift bridges so that their horses could negotiate those watercourses.

Bruce must have watched them take that course, and realised where they were going to spend the night. He had some thinking to do, and would have called his captains to him, James included, to debate the various possibilities that lay before them.

24 June 1314

There are only a few hours of darkness in the Scottish midsummer night. Bruce must have looked down towards the English positions on the carse, and as the light started to fail there would have been many, many pinpoints of light dotting up here and there, spreading out and covering the low ground between the Scots and the silvery line of the Forth. The English would have lit many campfires to cook their evening meal. James must have stood at Bruce's side, along with his other captains, and they would have spoken about the events of the previous day.

Bruce had chosen his army's position carefully. A track ran to its rear, by Gillies Hill where his camp followers were stationed, skirting the Touch Hills (pronounced 'two-ch', the emphasis on the first syllable) and continuing over into the valley of the River Carron. Once in this valley, men could turn west into the foothills of the Highlands, a rough landscape where the English could not follow. If they turned east they would come out of the hills into the countryside round Denny, and there they would be behind the English and could harass them and cut off their supply lines. Bruce could leave the field and retire to fight again. This track still exists, today called the 'Tak me Doon' road. It is narrow though driveable, coming out into the valley at the Carron Bridge Inn.

To fight would mean a pitched battle against many times the Scots'

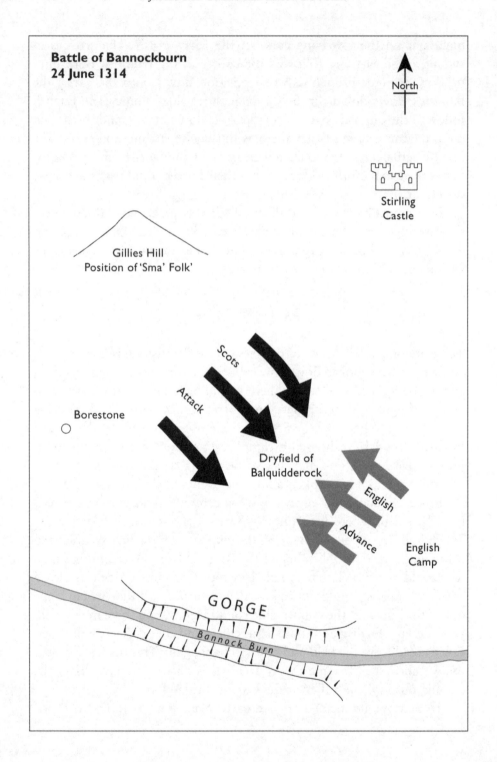

Battle of Bannockburn
24 June 1314

North

Stirling
Castle

Gillies Hill
Position of 'Sma' Folk'

Borestone

Scots

Attack

Dryfield of
Balquidderock

English

Advance

English
Camp

GORGE

Bannock Burn

numbers. Bruce did not want to risk the lives of his men in a vainglorious attack.

Just then, a rider came in from the English camp. It was Sir Alexander Seaton, a Scot who had been fighting with the English. He told Bruce:

> My Lord King, now is the time, if you ever mean to win Scotland. The English have lost heart; they are discomfited, and expect nothing but a sudden and open attack. I swear, on my head, that if you attack them in the morning you will defeat them easily and without loss.

This is interesting for many reasons. The English had turned up expecting that no matter the situation they came across in Scotland, it would be a walkover. They had been put to flight twice that first day and their usually unshakable belief in their own superiority had taken a dent. It also speaks volumes to me regarding the psyche of some Scots. This man Seaton had sided with the English. When he saw the unrest in their camp he decided to come back to his own people. He would never have done so, of course, if it had still seemed that the English would easily win. I feel that not too much has changed in 700 years. Those who shout most about keeping Scotland in a Union with England would probably be the first to change horses in the middle of the stream if it looked like Scotland was going to take its rightful place as a nation state again, claiming that they had been patriots the whole time.

Bruce turned and, set-faced, looked to his captains. He never wanted to risk everything in a pitched battle, but perhaps the time had come when he could justify that risk. The future of Scotland hinged on his next question. He asked his captains whether they should fight. He looked round their faces, and one by one they nodded. He looked at James. He nodded too. Barbour tells us that they told Bruce, 'We shall not fail for fear of death, nor flinch at any suffering till we have made our country free.'

So be it then. At first light the Scots would take on the mightiest fighting machine in Christendom. James, like the other commanders, went back to his schiltrom and told his men that they should prepare for battle.

The English down in the carse had a sleepless night. After the Scots' success they were worried that they could be attacked at any time, so they stood to arms. No man wanted to sleep knowing that he could awake to a melee, or for that matter, never wake at all.

Bruce must have spent some time in thought, deciding what tactics he should use. He gave his orders to the Scots. He would hold his division back, but the other three schiltroms, under his brother Edward, James and Randolph, would launch the attack as it grew light.

James would have walked through his men, offering words of encouragement, giving a nod and a wry grin to those who had shared adventures with him over the last seven years. There must have been many Scots inured to hard fighting after the long years of war, ready to test all in this coming crisis point in their nation's destiny.

As said, the Scottish midsummer nights are very short. Weather experts have assessed that both 23 and 24 June 1314 were dry and sunny, so there would have been no cloud cover to stall the onset of dawn. Probably around 3.30 in the morning, the first lightening of the sky would have been noticeable. The Scots were facing the English positions, the Ochil Hills on the other side of the River Forth starting to emerge clearly from the gloom. Bruce called for quiet and said a few words to his countrymen. Part of that speech was as follows:

> Those barons you can see before you, clad in mail, are bent upon destroying me and obliterating my kingdom, nay, our whole nation. They do not believe we can survive. They glory in their warhorses and equipment. For us the name of the lord must be our hope of victory in battle.

Bruce created some new knights, chivalry stating that a battlefield was one of the better places to carry out such an honour. Barbour tells us that James was knighted at this point, although there has been some debate regarding this ennoblement. It seems strange that someone who had spent several years carrying forward the Scottish cause, and who came from a family steeped in nobility, would not have been knighted before this point in his career. There had been times when James was in command of knights during battles, Brander being an example of this, and it would be odd if he was not at the least their equal in rank. The truth is, we don't know for sure, but one theory is that James was promoted to 'knight banneret' at Bannockburn. This honour can only be conferred on the field of battle, and its symbolism would have involved James handing his knight's pennant to his king, whereupon Bruce would have used his sword to slash off the double points of this flag to convert it to the square pennon of the banneret.

Bruce would have made a final eye contact with each of his captains, and then he gave the fateful order, and the schiltroms began to move forward in the early morning light.

Bruce's brother was the first to move. Edward led his division forward. It was only right that as the king's brother he should have the honour of beginning the fight. To his left, slightly behind in echelon, marched the schiltrom of Randolph, and to his left in turn and a little behind again, came the schiltrom of James. Randolph had been stationed closest to St Ninians on 23 June, but today, in this advance, he and James had swapped sides.

Bruce must have stood before his division at the Borestone, watching his army march down the slight gradient with its forests of spears outstretched. He had put the wheels in motion. Not only his, but Scotland's future would be decided this day. The army came forward, crossing the dip of land where Clark Street stands today, and as it rose again, would have been visible to the English forward lines on the edge of the carse. Trumpets must have sounded in the English camp, and there would have been a flurry of activity as they prepared to meet the Scots in battle.

The English heavy cavalry divisions, 10 in all, moved into their positions and came forward to meet the Scottish threat. They came up the 50 ft or so of rise onto the Dryfield of Balquidderock, which, as the name suggests, the English thought was perfectly suited for the cavalry battle they expected to fight.

Bannockburn High School stands on the Dryfield today, but there is still much open ground, and walking there it is easy to imagine that day in 1314. Stirling Castle rises on its rock, just as it did then. You can look over to the Abbey Craig, the only change there being that the National Wallace Monument now graces its summit. The ground there is firm. Perfect cavalry terrain, and you can see why the English horse moved forward to take advantage of the ground. You can also still see the restrictions of that ground. Balquidderock Wood, familiarly called

'Bluebell Wood' by the locals, now graces the slope that the English advanced up onto the Dryfield from the carse.

As the two lines began to form up facing each other, Bernard de Linton, the Abbot of Arbroath, held aloft the Brecbannoch of Saint Columba, the name meaning 'Little Speckled House' in the Gaelic. This item, which can be seen in the Museum of Scotland in Chamber Street in Edinburgh, was one of our most important religious icons. As it was held aloft, the Scots dropped to their knees, reciting the Lord's Prayer and commending their souls to God.

King Edward II of England had watched the Scots advance, astonished that this 'rabble' should actually come onto the field of battle. He turned to his commanders and exclaimed, 'What! Will those Scots fight?' When the Scots knelt to pray, he thought he had his answer. He added, 'They kneel to ask for mercy!'

Yet another renegade Scot, Sir Ingram de Umfraville, who was standing at King Edward's shoulder, informed him, 'You are right. They ask for mercy, but not from you. They ask it from God for their sins.'

The Scots rose, levelled their spear points at the English lines before them, and marched on in good order.

The English heavy cavalry, starting to mass on the Dryfield, came forward at the trot, expecting to ride over the comparatively lightly armed Scots. But the three schiltroms came on, filling the gap between the two armies, and the English heavy horse never had time to lumber forward into anything resembling a charge.

Heavy cavalry needs room to deploy; to gain momentum to smash into and crush their enemies under metal-shod hooves. The Scots never gave them space to do that; their spears formed an impenetrable barrier, and the English found themselves hemmed in. What was worse was their realisation that the rear ranks of horse, and the many thousands of foot soldiers behind, were still pushing on, eager to begin to fight, and they could not turn to find the room to reform.

The three Scottish schiltroms formed one long impenetrable barrier, with the English left hemmed in by the gorge of the Bannock Burn.

The Scots stabbed and stabbed with their long spears, aiming more at the horses than their riders. Wounded animals, desperate to escape that forest of spear points, threw the steel-clad knights on to their backs from six feet above the ground. They would lie stunned from the fall, prone to the trampling hooves of their fellows. Here and there a Scot would dart through the front ranks to stab at shoulder joint or eye slit of any Englishman trapped by the weight of his armour.

Where was James during this entire affray? Did he carry a weapon and lead by example, or stand a little behind the front line, shouting orders, bolstering his men?

Probably a bit of both.

I can see him, sword in hand, shouting encouragement, and occasionally using his martial fervour to cut a slash here and there.

From his Borestone position, Bruce tried hard to play a waiting game. He watched the drama unfold on the lower ground of the Dryfield, some half a mile in front of his command position. He knew that the three schiltroms fighting together had contained the English, but he also knew that his army was heavily outnumbered and that the English had weapons that he needed to counteract.

Bruce had been present at Wallace's ill-fated battle at Falkirk in 1298, and had seen how the schiltroms there had held charge after charge of heavy horse, but how the massed longbows of the English had torn gaps in them that had eventually led to their collapse, and how many thousands of Scots had died. He waited to see if something similar would be deployed by the enemy here, and so held back his light cavalry under Keith the Marischal, along with the men of his own schiltrom.

The English were no fools of course, and there were many soldiers of great experience in their ranks. They knew that they had to extricate their forces from the situation they found themselves in. Orders were barked, and the many divisions of archers in the English rear made their way to the right of their forces. As stated, the gorge of the Bannock Burn hemmed in the English left, the gorge forming the edge of the Dryfield of Balquidderock. There was some free ground to the right, a hummock of rising ground, near where Broom Road stands today. The archers made their way through the rear ranks of their own forces and started to mass on this rise.

Bruce watched them, but knew he had to wait a little till they were fully in position. I'm sure James was glancing to his left, watching the archers gather. He knew that with the Scots thickly deployed, all those archers had to do was fire into the mass, and the schiltrom would collapse, with the Scots dropping like flies.

The archers started to unleash their deadly hail, piecemeal at first, but growing heavier. Bruce knew the time had come. He signalled to Keith and his horsemen.

Keith moved them forward. He would have pointed at the heart of the body of archers, and with a roar, the horsemen would have urged their steeds forward down the slope. It took a few minutes for them to cross the intervening ground, but the English probably did not perceive the danger at first, continuing their firing at the Scots already engaged.

Even if they saw the horsemen approach, and turned to aim their bows, it would be difficult for them to pick the riders off, swift moving as they were.

The Scots light horse crashed into the first ranks of archers, sweeping them aside and underfoot, the riders swiping left and right with their swords, axes and maces. Archers wore little or no armour, and they had no defence once the Scots horsemen were upon them. Many were slain; the rest ran, making their way back towards the mass of their own army. There they found that the ranks would not open to let them through, and they were threatened and pushed back for some reason, and left to their fate.

Keith's horse were now free to harass the English flanks or pick off any stragglers.

James would have watched the destruction of the threat of archery, and I'm sure he and the rest of the Scots must have breathed a huge sigh of relief. Bruce knew that he had annulled a great danger to his men, and perhaps somewhere in the back of his mind he had an inkling that the day could now be won. Now that the archers were gone, he could commit his own schiltrom. At his command they levelled their spear points and marched forward.

When they reached the three schiltroms already committed, Bruce's men assimilated themselves into the ranks, Barbour telling us that they fought as one huge schiltrom. They began to chant, 'On them, on them, they fail!' They pushed forward with little half steps, shoving at the huge contained mass of Englishmen. The English could not move back to escape the spears as their fellows were pushing in from behind, unaware of what was happening to the front ranks. This situation continued for some time.

The Scots may have contained the English, but the odds were still very great, and although they were slowly killing their foes, there were many English untried and unbloodied beyond, the bulk of the army never having faced a Scot. And the Scots were growing tired with their exertions. Somewhere in the mass stood James, urging his men on.

Back on Gillies Hill, the many Scots who were untrained, and warriors come too late, and mere camp followers and the like, looked forward the mile or so to this scene. Perhaps they perceived the impasse that their fellows now found themselves in, or perhaps they were just itching to take part in the fight and that is what drove them to take action.

They used blankets on poles to create makeshift banners, grabbed what weaponry was available and came forward at the run, yelling slogans. The English saw another division of Scots appearing over the skyline, fresh and ready to continue the fight. At the sight of it, they wavered and fell back a little.

These charging Scots became known to history as the 'Sma' Folk', the name simply a Scots corruption of the term 'Small Folk'. This is a reference to the fact that although they were not part of the original main force, they were determined to take part in the fight for the liberation of their country.

They joined ranks with their fellows, and the chant went up again, 'On them, on them, on them, they fail!' The whole Scots army took heart and, though growing exhausted, redoubled its efforts. The English line began to waver, and the Scots found themselves moving forward in fits and starts, people tumbling away from the spear points.

King Edward II realised that his army was beginning to crumble and his commanders, alarmed, advised him to leave the field of battle for his own safety. He rode off in the direction of Stirling Castle, accompanied by no less than 500 of his knights. Some victorious Scots pursued him and managed to slay his horse, but another was quickly found and the English king was led away. Sir Giles d'Argentan, the third knight of Christendom, informed King Edward that he was not used to fleeing any fight, and reined his horse round to single-handedly charge the Scots. He was soon impaled on the spear points and brought down, never to rise again.

Seeing their king leave the field, the English resistance collapsed, and the battle degenerated into a series of running fights, many of the enemy veering off the field to their left and heading for the gorge of the Bannock Burn. Panic had taken hold, and many stumbled over the steep muddy sides of the gorge, knowing that the Scots were running at their rear, hungry for blood.

Many fell, and others fleeing fell upon them. Hundreds began to die, crushed under the press, and anyone who managed to rise was slain by pursuing Scots.

English chroniclers recalled the horrors that overcame their army as they tried to flee. The *Scalacronica* states that the English 'recoiled upon the ditch of the Bannock Burn, tumbling over one another.' The *Life of Edward* II states, 'While our people fled, a certain ditch entrapped many of them, and a great part of our army perished in it.' And the *Lanercost Chronicle* says, 'Many noblemen and others with their horses fell into this ditch because of the great press of men behind them. Some got away with difficulty, but many never extricated themselves.'

These accounts, along with the oldest drawing of the battle, contained within the *Scotticronicon* from the 1440s, show that the battle must have been fought on the Dryfield, the Bannock Burn and its gorge clearly depicted to the south of the main scene of conflict. All reports of the battle being fought out on the carse, where the Scots could easily have been outflanked, must be dismissed.

The battle of Bannockburn had been won and lost. As the realisation that the invader had been routed sank in, the jubilation among the Scots must have been immense. But the slaughter would continue, not just for hours, but for days, as ordinary Scots attacked the fragments of the English army as they wended their sorry way to the Border.

Bruce's authority shows in the fact that he was able to call James to him as soon as the main fight was over. It would have been easy for the Scots to take off in search of plunder, but Bruce knew there were still many thousands of English unblooded, and although they had been beaten as an army, these many individuals still posed a threat. He kept a tight rein on the discipline of his forces. There was a huge mopping-up operation in place, but Bruce had a special task for the Lord of Douglas.

The Aftermath

Bruce would have seen King Edward and his large retinue leave the field. The English king made his way toward Stirling Castle, where many demoralised English soldiers followed. They were seen scrambling on and about the castle rock, hoping for some kind of sanctuary. But the governor of the castle, Sir Philip Moubray, informed the king that the castle would soon be surrounded by the victorious Scots, and so shut the drawbridge against him.

King Edward and his 500 turned, and to escape the battle area, crossed the 'King's Park'. This, as its name suggests, was a hunting park of the King of Scots. It exists today, most of it covered by Stirling Golf Course.

Barbour tells us in his narrative that the English passed the 'Round Table'. By this, he was referring to the strange geometric grassy mound in the Royal Gardens under Stirling Castle, adjacent to the modern Dumbarton Road. Another link that suggests the legendary King Arthur was of the 'Strathclyde' Britons and was based in Scotland.

Taking this route, King Edward skirted the rear of the Scottish army, and the English galloped on, heading east and making for the nearest fortress where they could rest away from the risk of capture. Bruce's castle-taking had been so successful that this was Dunbar Castle, some 60 miles distant, at the mouth of the Firth of Forth.

Bruce told James about King Edward's flight from the field. He told him to give chase, but warned him that he could spare only 60 horsemen to face the 500 that accompanied the English king. Although the enemy had been defeated and were demoralised, there were still huge groups in the area, like the many hundreds scrambling on the castle rock. Bruce could not spare too many men in case the English started to regroup. A large body had already made their way back to the English baggage train, and the victorious Scots had caught them there. The English had tried to make a last stand, but were routed in an action that was to be known as the Bloody Fauld (Fold).

James would have been told that Edward had headed off to the east. Perhaps he and Bruce guessed that Edward was making for Dunbar, or more specifically the castle of the Earl of Dunbar, who, although a Scot, was firmly on the English side.

Although pursuing 500 heavily armed knights with 60 light horse would have seemed like a pointless exercise to most, James showed his usual aplomb, shouted his orders, and then, spurring his horse, led his men in pursuit.

As the battle had begun at first light and the Scots had stood to arms during the night, James and his men had had little or no sleep. They had taken part in a huge battle against overwhelming odds and prevailed, and now they were galloping off on a pursuit that could last for many hours.

As they cleared the Torwood, James came across Sir Lawrence of Abernethy with 24 riders, coming to join the forces of the English. When informed of the outcome of the battle, Sir Lawrence immediately changed sides and his men joined James's pursuers.

I can understand why James would have welcomed any help, with the meagre numbers he had, but the behaviour of Abernethy appals me. He had been willing to battle with his fellow countrymen, but on hearing that the Scots had gained the upper hand, suddenly remembered the blood that was flowing in his veins.

Although fatigued, the Scots had the sense of victory to bolster themselves, and the English were probably as tired as they. They gained on Edward as he galloped along the high road to Linlithgow.

At Winchburgh the English halted to feed their horses. James instructed his men to do likewise. The two parties must have eyed each other. The Scots were outnumbered the best part of 10 to one, and an attack would have been suicidal. The English were confident enough to stop, but did not have the heart to attack. Either they were demoralised by the unexpected victory of the Scots or they feared that there were others in pursuit and did not want to get bogged down in a fight that might delay them.

As soon as they set off again, James was hot on their heels. He kept the Scots right behind them across the level cavalry country of Lothian. Occasionally an Englishman would fall behind his fellows and be cut down. In Barbour's expressive phrase, James pursued them so diligently that they 'could not stop for anus water to make'. The odd straggling Englishman was captured, but this would have depleted James's little force.

James hoped for a chance, a fateful error by the English, some mishap perhaps, that would give him an opening. But in the meantime he had to just keep the pursuit as close as possible.

Dunbar Castle grew close, and there was nothing James could do with the English knights clustered so close round their monarch. King Edward was admitted into the castle with a few of his men, then the rest of the English carried on, making for Berwick upon Tweed, which was still in English hands.

From Dunbar Castle, King Edward was able to take a boat south to Bamburgh and the safety of his own borders. There are quite a few 'if onlys' about this incident. If only the Scots had been prepared for the overwhelming victory they would achieve at Bannockburn. If only James had had a larger force to chase the English king. And if only the Earl of Dunbar had changed sides like Abernethy did when he heard of the Scots' resounding victory. The capture of the King of England would have brought Scotland the freedom she craved at once, and saved another 14 years of warfare and bloodshed, which occurred purely because of the English stubbornness and refusal to recognise Scotland's independence.

But no matter. James had carved a niche for himself. The King of England, with a force almost 10 times James's number, had refused to turn and face him during his flight. James had fought with valour and distinction on the field of battle, and he had behaved with chivalry, refusing to take any of the glory away from Randolph during his schiltrom's fight with the English cavalry.

He was still only 28 years old, and he was making his name as one of the most brilliant soldiers Scotland had ever produced.

CHAPTER NINE

The upper hand

MANY OF THE English knights that fled the field of Bannockburn made their way to Bothwell Castle on the River Clyde. Once they were inside and the gates locked, the Scots keeper, having been informed of their defeat, changed sides and handed them all over to the victorious Scots.

There were some illustrious names among these prisoners. The Earl of Hereford, King Edward II's brother-in-law, for one. His ransom alone returned Bruce's womenfolk from their prisons and cages, and others, like Bishop Wishart of Glasgow Cathedral, were able to see Scotland again. Well, Wishart did not really get to 'see' his beloved Scotland, as he was blind when he was finally released from captivity. But he had lived to 'see' his prodigy, Bruce, defeat the invaders and rout them entirely.

His tomb lies at the rear of the crypt of Glasgow Cathedral, forming a barrier between two of the little chapels. It is defaced and sadly neglected, with no marker. A state of affairs that should be rectified at once. He is one of the great names of the era of Wallace and Bruce and should be better remembered. He gave his all for Scotland, holding nothing back, and nothing should be held back when it comes to marking his last resting place with, at the very least, a plaque.

Bothwell Castle stands close to the town of the same name, above the Clyde. It is a majestic ruin, and probably the best-preserved early medieval castle in Scotland. Built by the Murrays, in later years it would become a property of the Douglas family. It is open to the public.

Bannockburn had been a huge victory for the Scots, and a hugely embarrassing and demoralising defeat for the English. But the hard fact is that it, constitutionally at least, changed very little. England was still not willing to concede that Scotland had any rights.

Bruce knew that the war was now going to be a drawn-out, protracted affair, and set out to decide how best to wage it to Scotland's benefit. He knew that he needed money, and what better policy than to

Farm sign at Skaithmuir north of Coldstream, scene of James' 'hardest ever fight'.

View from Roxburgh Castle, over the River Tweed towards the more modern Floors Castle.

Some of the remaining earthworks from James' manor house at Lintalee.

Sign from the farm at Wester Happrew, in the vicinity where James' captured Randolph.

James' tomb in St Bride's Kirk in Douglas.

What is reputed to be James' heart, inset into the floor of St Bride's.

Overhead view of James' effigy

St Bride's Kirk in Douglas.

The scant remains of Douglas Castle – the famous 'Castle Dangerous'.

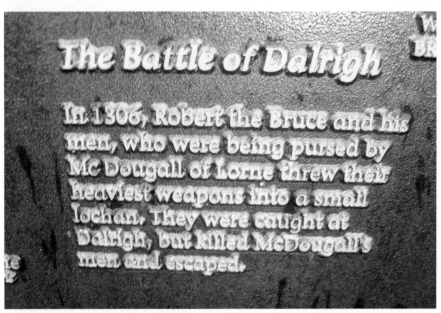

The Battle of Dalrigh

In 1306, Robert the Bruce and his men, who were being pursed by McDougall of Lorne threw their heaviest weapons into a small lochan. They were caught at Dalrigh, but killed McDougall's men and escaped.

Plaque marking the site of the Battle of Dalrigh.

View of the Pass of Brander from a shoulder of Ben Cruachan.

Walls of Carlisle besieged by James.

Cartmel Priory, James exacted tribute here.

Arms of James' companion, Sir Alan Cathcart, on a pillar in Paisley Abbey.

Remains of Knaresborough Castle, one of the places from which James exacted tribute.

Site of Dunaverty Castle at the southern end of Kintyre, where James took shelter with his king from pursuing forces.

Remains of Fountains Abbey. James was here during his invasions of England.

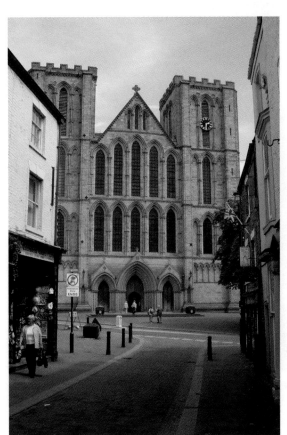
Ripon Minster. The townsfolk sheltered here from the invading Scots.

Modern plaque at the site of the Chapter of Myton.

The River Swale. Many of the English drowned on this stretch at the
Chapter of Myton.

Riveaux, where Edward II narrowly escaped the clutches of the Scots.

Sutton Bank. The Scots fought their way up the gradient at the Battle of Byland.

Tower of Richmond Castle, Yorkshire. James was here during his invasions.

View over Stanhope in Weardale, looking out from the Scots' positions.

St Hilda's Church in Hartlepool. James burnt the town several times.
(Note my motorcycle!)

Durham Castle. Durham was another town visited by the invading Scots.

The final resting place of Bruce's heart in Melrose Abbey.

Norham Castle. This place figured prominently in the Wars of Independence

The Castle of the Stars. The castle stands on a cliff above the village of Teba in Andalucia. This was the castle the Scots besieged before James' final battle in 1330.

Looking towards the Castle of the Stars from the area of James' final battle.

The monument to James and King Robert in the square at Teba. One side of the monument bears an inscription in English, the other side in Spanish.

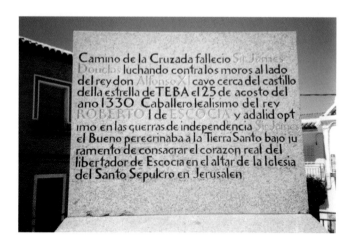

have England furnish that money? He would raid the northern counties of England while her great lords were in the south licking their wounds. And he had the perfect captain to carry out those raids. James had proven himself again and again, and so in August 1314, accompanied by Edward Bruce and a body of hardy veterans, he crossed the Border into Northumberland.

James and his men struck south, burning villages and farms en route to give warning to those they would meet ahead, the palls of rising smoke announcing the Scots' intentions.

The *Lanercost Chronicle* tells us:

> They burnt the towns of Brough and Appleby and Kirkoswald, and other towns here and there on their route, trampling down the crops by themselves and their beasts as much as they could. But the people of Coupland, fearing their return and invasion, sent envoys and appeased them with much money.

The travelled down into the bishopric of Durham, where they forced a 'tribute' from the clergy, ensuring that their lands and goods would not be prey to the Scots.

Durham Cathedral must have become a familiar sight to the Scots with their continued raiding. It still overshadows the town in all its medieval magnificence, the castle standing nearby. They carried on as far south as Richmond in Yorkshire. As you approach Richmond today, its hill-top castle with its huge central tower, protected by a bend of the River Swale, is still the overriding feature.

There they gathered prisoners for ransom, taking great numbers of livestock, and made their way back to the Border by following the valley of the River Swale up into the Pennines. From there they crossed the spine of the land, following the line of the modern B6270, and dropped down to the River Eden, taking its course towards Carlisle. There they slipped back over the Border unchallenged.

The booty from raids such as this kept the wheels of Bruce's war machine well greased, saving more depletion of an already war-ravaged Scotland. And Bruce had the grim satisfaction of knowing that the English were paying for the continuing war, which they had started.

This particular raid had gone very well. James had played his part, and Bruce decided to entrust him with the wardenship of the Border. From this time on, James was known as the Warden of the Marches, the 'marches' being the areas of the Border that ran alongside England. Normally there were three wardens, one each for the west, middle and east, who worked with their English counterparts in keeping the peace and good order. But these were not ordinary times, and it seems James was asked to keep a tight control over all the Borderlands.

These raids into England continued, and probed deeper south as the Scots' confidence grew. Bruce hoped that the constant raiding would bring the English to the conference table, where he could get them to recognise Scotland's independence. But it seems that King Edward II was not going to be persuaded.

There was a pattern to the raids. The north east of England was richer, more fertile country than the north west, which was more mountainous. Again and again the Scots would invade across the River Tweed, cross Northumberland and on into Yorkshire, demanding immunity from destruction in the form of money from English towns and villages. The Scots would strike far south as quickly as possible, so that warning would not reach their intended targets. They rode sure-footed little ponies called hobins. The riders were named after their choice of steed, and became known as hobelars. It is from these roots that the children's toy, the rocking horse, gets its name, 'hobbyhorse'.

The English would try and get the Scots to stand and give battle, but they were not interested. They merely wanted to raid, seeing that as a much better means to bring England to some sort of negotiation. The English were well armed and equipped, riding heavy war horses, but they were just not capable of moving at the fast pace the Scots could set, and so were helpless, the Scots never lingering long enough to be caught out.

Nearly every raid into England took on the form of a 'U'. The Scots would hurry south, delve into fertile English territory, generally taking an eastern route, then swing round and return north by the passes and river valleys cutting into the Pennine Hills, that long range that runs down the middle of England like a spine, and is indeed often called the 'Backbone of England'. They would then make their way back to the Border on the western side, the hills serving as a barrier to heavily-armed pursuers, and cutting down the chances of communication as to the Scots' movements, a knowledge that could have allowed the garrison of Carlisle, for instance, to waylay them.

Early in 1315, the Scots started to claim back the Lordship of Tynedale. It had been a fief of the Kings of Scots since the 1100s, and it seems many members of the populace were happy to switch their allegiance, so much so that they attacked their English neighbours. One line in the chronicle *Historia Aurea* struck me:

> The women went riding in a warlike manner, stealing the goods that their men did not care about, such as shorn wool and linen, and they carried them off.

A major shift in Scottish policy then took place. Bruce's brother Edward took a strong force over to Ireland in May 1315. Scotland was now assailing English rule on two fronts. While Scots incursions were plundering northern England, Edward Bruce was making inroads into the English hold on Ireland.

The rumour in English circles was that the Scots would assay to take Ireland, cross over to Wales, rouse the people there, and then make attacks on the deep untroubled south of England. James would then be able to raid further south and link up with his countrymen.

As previously mentioned, Scots preachers had spread the word that they had found an old prophecy of Merlin's, that after the death of 'le Roy Coveytous [meaning Edward Longshanks] the people of Scotland and the Welsh shall band together and have full lordship and live in peace together to the end of the world.' Probably propaganda of course, but it served to give belief to the Scots, and worry to the English.

King Edward II declared a truce with the Scots after the first post-Bannockburn raids south, but the people of England were not putting too much trust in their king after his various set-backs, and bought immunity from the Scots, truce or no.

In June 1315 the Scots again raided south over the Border. They rode hard and entered the city of Durham on the 29th of that month.

So stealthily had they come south, that the people were sleeping soundly in their beds. No warning of the Scots' approach had been given. Bruce based himself at Chester-le-Street, and sent James and his men on to Hartlepool to wreak destruction. On 1 July, a party of foraging

Scots caught the Prior of Durham unawares at his manor of Bearpark. He lost many possessions and many cattle.

When James reached Hartlepool, many of the townsfolk took to boats and sat off the coast, helplessly watching their town being ravaged. Unusually, he took many prisoners, and many womenfolk were led back to Scotland. His men ransacked all the surrounding countryside.

Why was Hartlepool treated so harshly?

It has been mooted that perhaps it was because Hartlepool had served as a gathering point and naval station for English invasions of Scotland. But it is my belief that it was because the town was once a Bruce fief, and when war had started with Scotland the town had not paid any of the monies Bruce felt he was entitled to, so James was given the task of teaching them a lesson.

The position of the town has moved a little. The medieval town was clustered round St Hilda's Church, but over the centuries the town has crept south round Hartlepool Bay. This church, still in use, was founded by an ancestor of Bruce. Several of Bruce's ancestors bore the Christian name 'Robert', so historians have used numbers to differentiate between them. St Hilda's was founded by the 'second' Robert Bruce in 1191 and his tomb has survived within, although St Hilda's literature states that the tomb is that of his grandson, the 'fourth' Robert Bruce. But careful analysis of the heraldry inscribed on the stonework shows us that it is indeed, the tomb of the earlier Bruce. The church is open to the public at certain times, and adjacent to it on the seashore is a remnant of the wall, containing the 'Sandgate', that was constructed to protect the inhabitants from Scottish deprevations after Bannockburn.

By 22 July, the Scots had crossed the Pennines and started a siege of Carlisle in the west. Carlisle was a walled, well-defended city, clustered round its powerful castle and cathedral. The castle and town gates were where Bruce's brothers' heads had been displayed. It would be a major loss of face for England to see one of its northern cities fall.

Sections of the walls still exist. To the west of the cathedral, above the railway tracks, there is a high and impressive stretch. The castle is well worth a visit, as is the Tullie House Museum in the town centre, which tells the history of Carlisle. The cathedral is a gem. Longshanks was there, and donated his litter to the place (it does not still exist, incidentally!) before marching on to his death at Burgh-by-Sands a little to the north west.

Carlisle had three gates, and each day between 22 July and 1 August, the Scots launched an attack on one or all of these. They were beaten back with losses on every occasion. The attackers were showered with darts and arrows, and the defenders on the walls pelted them with stones. So many stones in fact, that it is reported the Scots began to ask each other whether stones multiplied and grew within Carlisle's walls. Carlisle had a brilliant commander, Andrew Harclay, one of the greatest soldiers in England at that time. Over the coming years the Scots would see him as a worthy adversary and even imbue him with a grudging admiration.

The Scots set up a siege engine that could cast stones, near the Church of the Holy Trinity, but the defenders of the city had seven or eight similar machines inside the walls, besides other engines of war. We can only imagine the daily exchanges between the besiegers and besieged. Charges at the gates. Flying boulders. Flights of arrows. And the steady stream of casualties.

But the Scots did not just satisfy themselves with besieging Carlisle. One group struck south on 25 July to harass Penrith, its castle and the surrounding area. The ruins of Penrith Castle still stand in the town centre and are open to the public. James went south west of Carlisle and raided the area round Egremont. Egremont today is a pleasant little town just inland from the Cumbrian coast, clustered round the ruins of its castle, standing on its mound. William de Meschen founded the castle in the first half of the 1100s. De Meschen also founded the nearby Benedictine priory of St Bees. James raided this priory, taking some of its treasures back north. Part of the priory is still in use today, and has some old tombs and carven stones that are worth seeing. A body dating from the 1300s was discovered within one of these tombs in 1981. It was in a remarkable state of preservation, the flesh intact and traces of blood discernable! The priory is yet another place to visit that James himself would have known well in life.

James returned to the siege of Carlisle. In the interim the Scots had tried to assail the place with a belfry, a kind of siege tower, but it was very heavy and stuck in the soft ground, and the Scots were unable to move it forward. They had also tried filling the moat with various tied bundles of hay and corn and the like, but the water was too deep and all their efforts were simply swallowed up.

On 30 July, the main body of the Scots attacked the eastern walls of the city, creating a diversion while James and his men made an attempt to scale the western walls, probably the ones already mentioned that still stand to the west of the cathedral. James's party tried to secure a bridgehead on the walling, but despite their valiant efforts, they were beaten back. We are told that James suffered a wound of some severity during this fighting, but where exactly he was injured is not specified. Perhaps a broken bone from a missile or a stab wound? Two days later, on 1 August, Bruce decided to abandon the siege. The garrison of Carlisle felt confident enough under the leadership of Harclay to sally out from the protection of their walls and attack the Scots' rearguard, capturing some Scottish knights in the process.

The next we hear of James is in the following January. Early in 1316 the Scots decided to try and make a surprise attack on Berwick and free the Scots population from their English oppressors. So on 14 January a night assault was made by land and sea. But a bright, clear, moonlit night revealed the Scots' approach to the defenders and both attacks were repulsed, James apparently being one of those approaching by boat. The Scots did leave a body of men to keep an eye on the town and make sure that supply lines for the English were cut.

James seemed to be spending much of his time in the fastnesses of the vast Ettrick Forest, which covered much of the Scottish side of the Border in those days. He no doubt kept a body of fighting men with him, ready to respond to enemy action. The 10 years since Bruce had assumed the throne had produced many battle-hardened soldiers in Scotland. I'm sure James was able to hand pick a bunch that he could rely on, and the the men would similarly have trusted their commander. As Warden of the Marches he was be able to reach most Border areas under enemy threat at short notice.

Food was scarce in the Borderland, but scarcer still inside the walls of Berwick town. In October 1315 the governor, Maurice of Berkeley, wrote to King Edward of England, telling him that his men were ready to desert if pay and food were not forthcoming. It seems some rations managed to get through the Scottish blockade, but these did not last long, and by February the dark shadow of starvation was hovering over Berwick.

On St Valentine's Day, 14 February 1316, many of the garrison had had enough of their lot, and decided that they should go foraging across the countryside looking for food. There were many Gascons among these men (Gascony was part of King Edward II's domains), and they rode out under the leadership of one of their nobles, Edmund Cailhau, a chivalrous knight of wide lands in Gascony.

They rode up Teviotdale, the rolling farmland on either side of the River Teviot, and scattered out to take any cattle that they could find, driving the beasts before them. Sir Adam Gordon spotted some of the raiders from the village of that name, and galloped post haste to where James and his men were lurking. He told James that the cattle thieves were few in number, as he had seen only a fraction of the enemy that were actually out on the raid, and James did not think to doubt him.

James and his party set out at the gallop to find the raiders as they made their way back to Berwick. And find them he did. At Skaithmuir (it is pronounced 'skay-mur' by the locals), a few miles north of Coldstream, James suddenly came upon them, only to discover that he was faced by some 80 well-armed fighting men, along with some pages who were there to help with the cattle but were not armed. James had 40 followers with him. He had only a few seconds to make up his mind as to what he would do next. The countryside stretching out towards Berwick is known as the Merse. It is flat country, ideal for cavalry, but with little in the way of natural defensive features. There was a little ford nearby. James took his force towards it – a place where they could group and get ready for a fight. His famous white banner, with its blue band and three stars, was unfurled, a sign to the enemy that James was ready to come to battle.

James's trust in his men was unshakable, and after all, they had been heavily outnumbered at Bannockburn and had prevailed. To flee on Scottish soil was unthinkable. He had his king's trust and was Warden of those Marches.

Realising that their foes were few in number, the Gascons came on at the charge. They were desperate men, hungry, and probably eager to get to grips with their outnumbered opponents. Barbour's great poem tells us what happened next:

The Scotsmen bravely fought them back.
There one could see a cruel fight,
And strokes exchanged with all their might.
The Douglas there was full hard pressed;

But the great valour he possessed
So lent his men courageousness
That no man thought on cowardice.

The Scots fought with a dour effectiveness, hacking away with a brutal efficiency. James knew the quickest way to make his enemy lose heart was to seek out their leader and dispatch him. He cut his way through to Cailhau and engaged him in single combat in the middle of the bloody field. Cailhau was a brave knight, but he was no match for James Douglas. Slashing and cutting, James quickly brought him down, and then urged his own men on to greater exertions. Seeing their leader gone, the enemy began to crumble and the fight became a rout, with many slain in the pursuit. The cattle were all recovered.

Perhaps those slain by the Scots at Skaithmuir were the lucky ones. It was reported a few weeks later that the remaining members of the garrison at Berwick were dying of starvation at their posts on the walls.

From this time on, James would always go straight for the leader in any fight. He was a skilled warrior, and seemed to know no fear. He also knew that if he could get his enemy's resolve to collapse, he could save many Scottish lives.

Barbour, when writing his poem later in the 1300s, spoke to men who had fought with James. They reported that James had said that the fight at Skaithmuir was the hardest he was ever involved in, one where men fought with no quarter, giving their all. They had heard their accounts from James himself. How I would love to be able to sit with the man and have him tell me the story!

Barbour tells us that James retired to the fastnesses of Ettrick Forest after the fight at Skaithmuir. His name was on the lips of many Englishmen, who repeated the story of how he won against overwhelming odds, and spoke of him with awe.

Today, Skaithmuir survives in the name of a farm. At the entrance to the access road there is a small stream, and this may be the very one at which stood the ford that James used. It is a very small stream, hidden in the summer months by overgrowing grass. Perhaps drainage over the centuries has reduced its size. There is no other waterway in the area that really fits the bill, and it does not take a stream of much depth to impede charging horses.

I am indebted to locals for all the help they gave me in trying to locate the site of the battle. It was pointed out to me that one of the fields to the south east of the farm is known by the name of 'Greystane'. This might refer to a standing stone raised either to mark the site of the fight, or the spot where the dead were buried. The victorious Scots would have taken the time to bury the dead, or have hired people to do so, partly as a mark of respect and partly for purely hygienic reasons. Or perhaps the name is a corruption of 'gravestone'. Details to ponder at least. Certainly somewhere close to the farm is the site of the hardest fight that James ever had.

CHAPTER TEN

The 'Black' Douglas

AS STATED, the name of James Douglas began to be spoken by English-men with a deal of reverence. In those chivalric times it was a man's ability in arms that made him famous, and James certainly had an awe-some prowess on the field of battle.

As you can imagine, the constant mention of his name grated in some quarters. Sir Robert Neville of Raby, for example, grew irritated to hear it. Neville seems to have been a fighter of some renown. He had got into a war of words with Sir Richard Fitzmarmaduke, steward to the Bishop of Durham, apparently over who was the greater lord. The *Scalachronica*, a contemporary chronicle written by Thomas Gray, tells us that this rivalry culminated in a fight on the bridge at Durham Neville slew Fitzmarmaduke, and this deed incurred the wrath of King Edward II. The bridge where this fight took place has survived, and though Durham has three old bridges over the River Wear, this particular one is the town's Framwellgate Bridge, constructed in the 1120s. To try and placate his monarch, Neville went into military service and joined the garrison at Berwick. Neville must have been a snappy dresser too, or perhaps he just had a haughty demeanour, because he gloried in the moniker of 'The Peacock of the North'.

Hearing the garrison talk of James, he decided that he would show the upstart Scot who was the greater warrior once and for all. He had it shouted abroad that if James came anywhere near him with his banner unfurled, he, Neville, would attack him at once.

It was not long till the message was brought to James's ears in Ettrick Forest, and James, being James, decided that Neville should have the chance to make good his bold words.

James made his way to Berwick by night, and the next morning his standard was unfurled in view of the town walls. He also sent off a few of his men to set some of the surrounding buildings on fire, just in case Neville did not get a clear view of his intentions.

Neville gathered his followers and, unfurling his own banner, rode out at their head, and took up position on a nearby hilltop.

He must have had some kind of stratagem in mind, or have set up some kind of ruse, for Barbour tells us that he waited for a while because he believed that the Scots would break in search of plunder. Perhaps he thought that the men James had sent to set the neighbouring buildings ablaze would pillage and take what they could and not return to give fight.

James's band was too experienced for that, and his men returned at once. The Scots went into attack formation and, probably to Neville's surprise, rode straight for him on his hilltop position. Neville turned to his followers and shouted to them, 'We are the flower of England, and we outnumber those Scots. Let us attack them valiantly, for those Scottish yeomen have not the strength to withstand us!'

Neville's force spurred forward, expecting to easily overrun the out-numbered Scottish 'yeomen'. In the words of Barbour:

Then with a rush they made attack.
The sound of smashing spears arose,
As each on other dealt his blows,
And blood burst out from gashes wide,
The fight was fierce on every side,
For each man fought with might and main
To drive his foeman back again

In the middle of this melee, James came face to face with Neville and they set to combat. Heavy blows were exchanged, each man pushing himself to the limit, but as they traded blows, James's resolve and strength held sway. He was determined to bring his haughty opponent down.

The fateful blow came, and Neville, dead, hit the soil of Scotland.

James then yelled his battle cry, 'Douglas! Douglas!', and, praying to St Bride, charged into the surrounding Englishmen. His men, nothing loath, followed his example. The English began to buckle and then break, the Scots following at their heels, cutting and slashing. Neville's brother Sir Ralph was cut down, and the Scots captured some doughty fighters, including the Baron of Hilton.

When the field was clear, James allowed his men to loot the surrounding hamlets, which must have been galling to the helpless, watching garrison on the town walls. The Scots would also have stripped the slain of valuables and weaponry. Then they returned westwards to the fastnesses of the forest. James split all the booty taken between his men in acknowledgement of their valour, keeping none for himself. Gestures like this made his men love him. He told them how proud he was of their bravery and of their prowess in the fight for Scotland's freedom, and said they had the hearts of leopards. His constant vigilance to his men's well-being gave them eagerness for the fight and made them brave.

James's slaying of Cailhau, and now of Neville, the Peacock of the North, who had foolishly taken on one of the greatest soldiers Europe had ever produced with disdain, made him feared in England as if he were the very Devil of Hell. His name struck terror now wherever it was mentioned. Mothers in England began to scold their children with it. And a rhyme was coined: 'Hush ye, hush ye, little pet ye, the Black Douglas will not get ye.' There is a story that as one English mother rocked her child to sleep to this refrain, a calloused hand fell upon her shoulder, saying, 'don't be too sure of that...'

After the siege of Carlisle, it would be several years before King Robert the Bruce again struck south into England himself. He had two captains who could adequately carry out any tasks he needed doing across the Border: James Douglas and Thomas Randolph. Together or individually they were astonishing leaders of men, and basically capable of doing as they pleased with any forces sent against them. Only 10 years before, Bruce had been a hunted fugitive in his own country, James one of his few loyal companions, and Randolph coerced by the English. Now Bruce was able to leave the country in capable hands and go across to Ireland to help with his brother Edward's campaign there. Randolph accompanied him on this expedition, and so the control of Scotland was left in the hands of James and Sir Walter Stewart, Bruce's son-in-law.

In May 1316, Edward Bruce was crowned King of Ireland, and the campaign to wrest control of that country from English hands intensified.

James was now in his 30s. With his responsibilities in the Borders he felt that he needed a base of some sort in that area. It seems quite incredible to me that he chose the site he did, as it is so close to the English frontier. I would have thought he would have been wary of a night raid by a force of Englishmen, or even that he was on a possible line of invasion, but James probably had enough trust in his own abilities and those of his war band to feel a certain degree of safety. And of course, his name was one uttered with fear by the foe, so he may have felt that the English would not dare to try and assail him there.

The site chosen was Lintalee, some two miles south of Jedburgh. Jedburgh had its own castle, and it had been in Scots control since Bannockburn a few years before, but James preferred his own location. Perhaps he knew the lie of the land there and reckoned it would be a good place for the building of a fortified manor, or perhaps he thought the site's proximity to the Border would be galling to the enemy and make them try and carry out a foolhardy raid.

At any road, building work began. From his new position, he would be able to reach most areas of the Borders quickly when danger threatened.

With Bruce absent in Ireland, furthering both Scotland's and his brother's ambitions there, the English thought that they could perhaps take advantage of the situation and make inroads into Scotland. King Edward had appointed the Earl of Arundel the warden for England north of the River Trent. Arundel wanted to strike while Bruce was absent and show his king that he had picked the right man for the job. The band he gathered was no mere raiding party; the chronicles tell us that it amounted to many thousands of men.

Arundel issued an axe to each of his troops, and they had instructions to fell every tree as they crossed the Border. The Earl wished to destroy the forest round Jedburgh; the forest that had sheltered James and in which he had just put the finishing touches to his new home. Felling forests was not something new to invading English armies. They had done so some years previously, during their subjugation of Wales.

Arundel marched his army north in February 1317 and headed for the Border at Carter Bar, which today is the high point on the A68, where a monolith with 'Scotland' upon it marks the entry to the northern nation.

Word was brought hastily to James. He had prepared a house warming party for his men. I suppose most of us don't think about how old some of our everyday customs are, but 'house warming' is how Barbour refers to the feast that James had set up at Lintalee for his men.

This feast had to be hastily abandoned, as James ran out, calling for his men to arm themselves. As it was early in the year, James had not expected such a full-scale assault. He had perhaps 50 men-at-arms with him, and perhaps 150 archers. He led them on the road south to a place where he knew that the invaders must pass and he could put a stratagem to work. The road there ran through a glade with woodland on either side. Like a shield, the woodland tapered in. Eventually the trees almost reached the roadside. There were many silver birches there, slim, pliable trees, which are prevalent in Scotland. James had his men work fast, plying the branches together on either side, just enough to make a barrier impossible for horses to pass through. He had his archers take cover behind this screen, ready to assail the English when they came up. He ordered them to wait for his signal before they let loose their arrows, then took his 50 men at arms and blocked the road ahead.

The English vanguard appeared before them, but James held his men in check till he had the enemy exactly where he wanted them. At his cry of 'Douglas! Douglas!' the archers unleashed several volleys of arrows, taking out many of the Englishmen before them. James then led his men forward, and they ran into the English leadership. James, of course, had picked out the man he thought to be in charge of the vanguard, and he rode straight for him, determined to cut him down. The English captain, nothing loath, spurred forward to meet James, but the initial shockwave of Scottish riders tore many Englishmen from their saddles, the captain among them. James jumped from his horse, drew his dagger, and killed the man.

On top of his helmet, the dead man was wearing a hat trimmed with fur; James snatched this hat and took it with him as a token. The Scots men at arms cut down as many of the enemy as they could reach.

James then pulled his men back. For a few minutes his archers continued to fire into the enemy ranks before they too retired. The English had no idea how many were arrayed before them, so they collected the body of their leader and fell back toward their main host. The army then made camp for the night. The vanguard magnified the extent of the ambuscade that they had ridden into, telling how it was James, the Black Douglas, shouting the dreaded 'Douglas!' battle cry, who had fallen upon them with Scots innumerable and had slain their leader.

Meanwhile, word was brought to James that a party of some 300 men led by a clerk named Ellis had by chance bypassed his attack, and had taken up residence at Lintalee. Knowing that the main host under Arundel had come to a halt, unsure of its position, James with his characteristic need for action rallied his men and headed back to his headquarters.

He crashed through the doors to find that Ellis and his 300 had settled down to consume his house-warming dinner, and were already a little worse for wear from consuming the wine and spirits he had laid on for his men. They obviously assumed that James would have either fled or hidden from the host arrayed against him. The Scots drew their weapons and carved their way through the diners. Only a handful of the 300 managed to escape the slashing steel.

One captive was shown the fur-trimmed hat that James had taken from the captain he had slain; he identified it as that worn by Thomas Richmond, a knight from Yorkshire. Barbour has the dead man identified as the Earl of Richmond, but this could not have been the case, as the Earl was later to be captured by Bruce at the Battle of Byland in 1322.

The one or two survivors of the blood bath at Lintalee ran towards the Border, and happened across their encamped countrymen en route. They told how the Black Douglas had slaughtered their colleagues, and again the tale lost nothing in the telling. Arundel conferred with his lieutenants, and it was decided that the odds were too great and the country round about too roused and ready to defend itself for them to try and take their expedition further. They struck camp and headed back over the Border the next day.

Heading south from Jedburgh on the A68, the road following the meanderings of the Jed Water, you can see where Lintalee stood on a high spit on the right, about two miles south of the town. This spit drops to the Jed on one side and the Lintalee Burn on the other. There is a severe drop to the Lintalee Burn, running far below, and the place is completely defensible from that side. The gradient is still steep towards the Jed, but there would of course have been an approach path at that side. There is a private house on the site today, still bearing the name Lintalee.

In the garden of this house there is a large circular earthwork, with a central raised mound. As I said, it stands on private property, and that should be respected, but I wanted to at least tell you that vestiges exist of James's residence; the residence at which he butchered 300 of the invaders.

At this point in his narrative, Barbour tells us of 'Three Feats by Fifty'. This refers to three incidences during the Wars of Independence in which 50 Scots discomfited much larger forces. The one above regarding James's feat of arms against Arundel was the first, although a body of archers supported James and his fifty. The second one Barbour mentions is an incident in Galloway in which Bruce's brother Edward suddenly came across 1,500 English cavalry emerging from a heavy mist. Without waiting to see how many were actually before him, Edward spurred his men on and they smashed right through the English host. Reining round, they repeated the tactic again, and in the ensuing confusion, the English broke and galloped from the field.

The third incident was under the command of a leading Scottish knight, John de Soulis. In this incident de Soulis charged Andrew Harclay, he who had held Carlisle against Bruce and James, and a retinue of 300 men, and scattered them. Barbour then goes on to say:

> I need not tell the story here;
> For, who so wishes, he may hear,
> Young women, when they go to play,
> Sing it among them every day.

Obviously at the time Barbour's work was written, around 1370, these stories were well known among the ordinary populace of Scotland, and as Barbour tells us, young women sang of the deeds of de Soulis. All the detail has been lost to us. These wee snippets of everyday life in Scotland, the stories and tales of ordinary people, are mostly gone, leaving us the skeleton of history. It's a shame that Barbour did not realise that the rhymes should have been recorded, but perhaps he would have been shocked to know that people would be reading his works in the 21st century, and for many centuries still to come, long after such rhymes had been lost to human memory.

The English did make other attempts to win back their hold on Scotland. One such took place around the same time as James's adventures against Neville at Berwick and the fight at Lintalee. Englishmen from the north of their country, realising that their king was unlikely to stop any future Scots invasions, took it upon themselves to mount their own invasion by sea. They landed on the south Fife coast, somewhere near Inverkeithing. The local Scots immediately gathered to repel the English, under the command of the Earl of Fife and his sheriff, but took to their heels in fear as they saw them form up on the coast. Five miles away, at Auchtertool, the fleeing Scots met the armoured and armed Bishop of Dunkeld coming in the opposite direction.

When the bishop realised they were fleeing, he berated them and, lowering his lance, spurred his horse on to meet the enemy in single combat. The Scots watched him gallop off and, ashamed, turned and followed him. Taking courage from the bishop's example, the Scots drove the English back to the shore in confusion. Too many of the invaders tried to clamber into one boat, which capsized as it pulled out into the Firth of Forth, and many soldiers drowned in their armour.

1318 dawned, winter mellowed into spring, and campaigning season began again. The constant pressure for England to recognise Scotland's independence would never be let up. James had a friend and ally in Sir William Keith of Galston in Ayrshire. At a meeting, Keith explained that he had a relative through marriage who was in charge of a section of the walling of Berwick. He told Bruce that this relative, one Syme of Spalding, would be willing to help the Scots enter the town for a bribe. Syme's wife was a cousin of Keith, but Bruce felt that the story could be a ruse by the English to lead him into a trap. He considered for a while, and decided that it was worth the trying, but that the Scots should be wary that there was skulduggery afoot.

So who should lead this raid on Berwick? Bruce in his wisdom decided that James and Thomas Randolph should take joint command. There was now a real rivalry between these two, each always trying to outdo the other in feats of arms. But this rivalry was not born of jealousy; it was more a determination to succeed against the enemy and was not clouded by ill feeling.

Bruce informed them that they should lead a joint venture to capture the last town north of the Border still in English hands. It is reported by a writer, John of Tynemouth, that Syme asked for a bribe of £800 to allow the Scots to scale the walls 'un-noticed', and that he was later wrongly executed on a trumped up charge of plotting against Bruce. This latter part does not ring true as Bruce granted him lands in Angus for his troubles.

Keith gathered men from Lothian, and they made their way to the chosen meeting place near Duns, some 15 miles west of Berwick. James and Randolph arrived at the camp together, their two parties having met en route. Keith, Randolph and James hatched a plan between them. If they could gain the hoped-for entry into the town, some men would fan out through the streets while the main body sat with James and Randolph near the wall. They would wait till dawn was starting to break, and hopefully with surprise on their side there would be an almost bloodless coup.

On the night of Saturday, 1 April, they put their ladders in place and scaled the wall at the Cowgate. Syme of Spalding and his men did indeed turn a blind eye. The Scots dropped into the town, and once sufficient numbers had gathered, they were able to put their plan into operation. But before dawn had broken, some of the Scots who had scattered through the town were unable to resist the chance to gather loot, alerting the inhabitants to the fact that something was afoot, and the cry of alarm was raised.

We are told some fierce street fighting ensued. Some of James and Randolph's men ran to the strong castle of Berwick, but the gates opened and the garrison sallied out, pushing the Scots back. For a few minutes it was touch and go, the Scots starting to break under the pressure. But then Keith, who had rallied his own men, came to the rescue, smiting mightily. Keith fought with distinction that day, greatly increasing his renown, and adding his name to the list of brilliant young captains with whom Bruce was able to surround himself.

Eventually resistance died down as opponents were slain, or simply surrendered. The remnants of the castle garrison managed to fight a rearguard action, and they safely re-entered the castle gates, slammed shut the doors and dropped the portcullis. But the town at least was back in Scottish hands, and now Bruce was the master of the last piece of the jigsaw. Other than the few Englishmen in that castle, all of Scotland was under his sway.

The castle gallantly held out for another 11 weeks before starvation took its toll and the fortalice was surrendered to the Scots.

James's father had been captured at Berwick and led from the castle in chains. James had started out on his chosen career determined to win back his heritage, and he had achieved much more that he could have ever dreamed of. Now he had taken the town and fortress where his father had been humbled. There must have been a grim satisfaction at a job well done.

The town of Berwick changed hands many times during the turbulent days of warfare between Scotland and England. Eventually, after yet another incursion in 1482, it became an English town. I should point out that it is an English town in name only, because Berwick stands on the north bank of the River Tweed and so geographically is in Scotland. Hopefully this situation will be rectified at some point in the future.

When it fell into English hands for the last time, Berwick became a bastion, heavily defended against the Scots. In the time of Elizabeth I of England, new walls were built. You can still walk round the historic old town on these walls, and one sizable length remains from the time of the Wars of Independence, running from the remains of the castle down to the River Tweed.

The town's railway station stands on the site of Berwick Castle. Although in ruins now, it was relatively complete in the 1800s. When the age of steam arrived and the railway came to Berwick, much of the castle was demolished to make way for the new platforms. It is unfortunate that the people in power in those days did not make much of an allowance for conservation, especially for a site that played such a prominent role in the history of both Scotland and England. Crossing the bridge over the lines and going down the stairway, you will notice that there is a hanging sign proclaiming you are at the site of the Great Hall of Berwick Castle. Standing on the platform there lets you look across the track to what little remains of the once mighty fortification. From those ruins you can see the remnants of the medieval walls running to the river.

It is always nice to visit such remains when you know the tales of what passed there before. I feel that walking the landscape makes the story come alive, and allows you to put everything in perspective.

CHAPTER ELEVEN

Devastation and declaraton

NOT LONG AFTER the fall of Berwick, the Scots launched their largest raid yet into northern England. In early May 1318, they struck south in two parties, their target being Yorkshire. The leaders were James and Randolph. They bypassed Durham, which had already bought immunity from their raiding. Seeing such a large force pass south would have left that city in no doubt as to what would happen if it did not keep up future payments. The western group crossed the River Tees into Yorkshire at Barnard Castle (the castle which gave the town its name still stands) while the eastern crossed into the shire at Yarm, after again sacking Hartlepool and its environs.

The western group stuck Richmond and sent raiding parties into Wensleydale, then on to the next major town of Ripon. There the population crammed into the minster in the hope that God would protect them from the ravages of the Scots. But it seems that divine intervention was not forthcoming, as they negotiated immunity for their town by promising to pay 1,000 marks. The Scots took six hostages to ensure that Ripon would keep its word, and it seems the town did indeed try to renege on the deal, as King Edward of England later ordered Ripon to pay the money so that the hostages could be returned. Ripon Minster is still a fully functioning place of worship today. Work was begun on today's building in the 1100s, and the crypt of the earlier Anglo Saxon church of St Winfrid can still be visited, this crypt dating from 680AD. As I stood in this ancient crypt I wondered if James was ever down here, looking at it as I did. Certainly it is an ancient remnant of early Christian worship that makes Ripon worth a visit if you are in the area.

The Scots then made for Fountains Abbey, where another tribute was gathered, but this did not stop the Scots from making the abbey a base and raiding the surrounding manors and granges. Fountains today is an impressive ruin. In its heyday it was a very wealthy establishment. I would love to have seen this place when it was in its full glory, full of tombs, statues and colourful carvings, sitting as it does in its little vale. Unfortunately you can't just pull up and have a look at it. You really have to park and pay to walk down and see this place, as it is well hidden from the surrounding roads, and it is only when you are really upon it that it comes into view.

The eastern party of Scots galloped down the Vale of York, making for Northallerton, which was ravaged and burned. They then pushed on south for Boroughbridge. There they took the corn from the king's granaries and burned the town.

The two parties came together at Knaresborough. There they wreaked havoc. The *Lanercost Chronicle* tells us that only 20 houses were left standing in the town once the Scots had set fire to it. In the centre of the town, Knaresborough Castle stands high on its cliff above the River Nidd. It was built around 1100, was remodelled by Edward I and Edward II, although it is ruined today. This building would have been familiar to James. The Scots also scoured the surrounding woodlands for folk hiding their cattle or possessions. It was reported that the Scots camped in the parish of Pannal, and then they burned that too. They made raids out in every direction, taking anything that would not be too cumbersome to carry on the journey home. The Scots crossed the Pennines, burning each parish they passed through. Once in the west, they raided Preston and sallied right out to the coast. Then it was Lancaster's turn, and much damage was done to the town – and not only to the town, as it seems almost every parish in the whole shire suffered a visit from the Scots. Sated, they finally turned their horses' heads to the north and home to Scotland.

Unlike English invasions of Scotland, which were begun in the name of conquest, the Scots had no intention of holding onto any English property. Their raids were made to apply pressure on the English to recognise Scotland's right to sovereignty. The raids could be stopped immediately. All England had to do was admit that Scotland was a nation state, and the trouble would cease. But King Edward II would not do anything to help the people of his northern counties. He was not prepared to give up Scotland, obviously hoping that his fortunes would change and he would be able to reassert his claim on the country, using full-scale invasion to subjugate her.

1318 had been a good year for the Scots in northern England. They seemed unstoppable, the English helpless to stop them doing as they pleased. But things had not gone so well in the Irish campaign. In October, Edward Bruce, King of Ireland, with a predominantly Scottish army, was defeated at Dundalk and slain.

Edward had been headstrong. A brilliant leader of cavalry, but lacking his brother's tactical genius and knack for self-preservation. He had apparently marched to Faughart, near Dundalk, with his army split into three groups. These three marched so far apart that there was no real contact between them. When the leading group marched into an Anglo-Irish army, the superior numbers easily overcame them. The Anglo-Irish were able to regroup and use the same tactics against the second group, then the third. Somewhere amidst this carnage, Edward Bruce was cut down.

Edward's body was mutilated. His head was sent to King Edward II, and his body was quartered. A Dublin chronicler tells us that his 'heart, hand and one quarter was sent to Dublin to be put on public display, the other quarters of his body were sent to other places.' Even though there is little doubt that Edward Bruce's body was scattered to the winds, there is a strong tradition that the English got the wrong man, coupled with a tradition in Faughart that Edward was buried in the local grave-yard. In the mid 1800s a burial stone was marked as his grave.

King Robert the Bruce had now lost every one of his brothers to the English. Over and above that, Edward had been his heir. It must have caused much soul searching on Bruce's part, but he knew that personal grief could not be allowed to get in the way of his role as king, or to cloud his judgement. The push to win Scotland's complete independence would carry on no matter what.

The succession in Scotland had to be secure, so at the end of 1318 it was decided that the heir to Bruce's throne would be his grandson, Robert. Bruce's daughter Marjory had died in 1316 after falling from her horse. A cairn marks the spot, standing opposite the Chivas building in Paisley. Marjory is buried in Paisley Abbey. Robert was eventually to be the first of the Stewart line of kings, taking his throne as Robert II.

It was decided that if Bruce died, Randolph would be the regent in the minority of the young Robert. This was not too much of a surprise, as Randolph was Bruce's nephew and of the blood royal, and had proven himself as a capable statesman as well as a warrior. But a rider was added which said that, should Randolph die, the regency would fall on the shoulders of James, Lord of Douglas. This was a singular honour. James had risen to the top rank. He was a man capable of holding the reins of power in Scotland, and the trust that went hand in hand with that honour.

There were by this time, as you can imagine, many disaffected people in the north of England, and probably King Edward's most voracious opponent was Thomas, the Earl of Lancaster. There had been many hot words between these two, but it seems that when the Scots took Berwick back into their fold they created a certain harmony among the English. Lancaster joined forces with his king to try and win Berwick back. Berwick was the largest and most prosperous town in Scotland at that time, and the English were especially determined to hold on to it.

The King of England himself led an army of some 8,000 north to lay siege to Berwick. His father had taken Berwick easily and had slaughtered the population, so the English were confident that they would be able to regain the town to use as a base for continued inroads into Scotland.

Bruce had placed Berwick under the command of his late daughter's husband, Walter Stewart. Stewart had fought with great distinction at Bannockburn. It must have been quite a company when the likes of James, Randolph, Keith and Stewart got together to discuss their experiences.

Bruce made sure that Berwick was fully defended, not just with quality fighting men, but with the latest in engineering. John Crab, a Fleming of great skill, made engines to hurl stones and fireballs. Interestingly, Barbour states that the Scots had everything they needed, except 'gynnis for crakis'. By this he meant cracker-guns, i.e. cannon. Early versions of cannon began to appear around this time, and although the first examples were unwieldy and probably about as dangerous to those doing the firing as those fired upon, James and his like were to see in their lifetime the very first examples of the instrument that would eventually make their type of warfare obsolete.

The English appeared outside Berwick and, realising that there would be a concerted effort to hold the walls against them, began to dig in, and to raise earthen ramparts round their own camp to defend themselves against any kind of sally from within the town. This done, they unfurled their many banners, and on 8 September 1319 the assault began.

Ladders were placed against the walls, but the Scots cast them back, and many Englishmen fell to their deaths. There were showers of arrows exchanged, and we are told that the English host was large enough to completely encircle the town walls.

Walter Stewart rode from point to point with a party of reinforcements to bolster the defenders whenever it began to look like the English could make a breakthrough.

The English brought a ship across the River Tweed, and it closed in towards the town walls. The walls would not have been so heavily defended where there was water, as it would have seemed impossible to breach them there. This ship had been specially adapted, with a drawbridge of sorts affixed halfway up the mast. The general idea was to sail the ship in to the walls and lower this drawbridge onto them, whereupon a host of heavily-armed besiegers would storm their way into the town. The ship assayed to close in by the old town bridge (the many-arched bridge that now crosses the Tweed there, built in the time of James VI, marks the general area where it stood) but the defenders put up a very concerted defence, and forced it back again and again. Eventually, with the tide receding, the ship began to founder in the mud. As soon as there was dry ground between the walls and the ship, men ran forth, and with blazing torches, set the ship ablaze. Many Englishmen were killed, and the rest made their getaway across the sand and rocks.

When the main English host saw the ship ablaze, they ran towards the Scots out on the riverbanks, determined to cut them off and force an entry at the gate from which they had emerged. Just in time, the Scots rushed back in and the gate was barred.

At the end of that first day's fighting the English retired to their camp to lick their wounds.

When he had first heard that the English were approaching the Border, Bruce had called for James and Thomas Randolph, and instructed them to do what was necessary to relieve Berwick. Neither of these stalwarts was interested in risking a single Scot's life unnecessarily, and they knew it would be suicidal to take on the 8,000-strong English host in the field, never mind attacking them in their rampart-surrounded camp. But they knew the surest way of unsettling the English and making them look over their shoulders was to bypass them and go raiding in northern England.

So they made their way into England by the west march, and then crossed the Pennines, directly south of the besiegers of Berwick. I'm sure that the Scots would have set fire to everything they could, letting the smoke palls rise, making the army sitting outside Berwick wonder what was happening to their homeland. The rumour spread that the Scots were planning to capture Edward's queen, Isabella, who was based at York with the English administration.

James and Randolph left a trail of destruction in the Vale of York, heading to Northallerton, and then on towards Boroughbridge. A spy then revealed himself to Archbishop Melton of York, and confessed that the Scots were coming to kidnap the queen. He also said that he could lead the townsfolk to where the Scots were lying in wait. For safety, the Queen of England was removed to Nottingham.

A call to arms went out from York, demanding that all capable citizens should march out to Myton-on-Swale and teach the Scots a lesson. Most of the able-bodied fighting men from the area were already at Berwick with their king, and so Archbishop Melton gathered together a motley crew of churchmen, peasants and townsfolk. English chronicles claim they were 20,000 in number (probably an exaggeration). On 12 September this force marched out to do battle with the greatest soldiers in Europe...

James, Randolph and their men were camped out in a field on the west bank of the River Swale, near its confluence with the River Ure. Archbishop Melton, with his silver crucifix held aloft as a standard, approached with his army, many churchmen to the fore, with choir boys singing. He obviously wished to emulate his predecessor, Archbishop Thurstan, who had had religious artefacts carried before his army when he defeated the Scots at the Battle of the Standard at none-too-distant Northallerton in 1138.

The army came to the village of Myton and crossed the River Swale by the bridge there. The Scots, seeing them approach, set ablaze three piles of damp hay that were in the vicinity. The English marched on through the thick smokescreen that the burning stacks caused, emerging at the far side to find the Scots before them in full battle order. These men were the veterans of many years' fighting alongside Bruce, veterans of Bannockburn, and had spent the last few years raiding into northern England. Many had probably seen action in Ireland too.

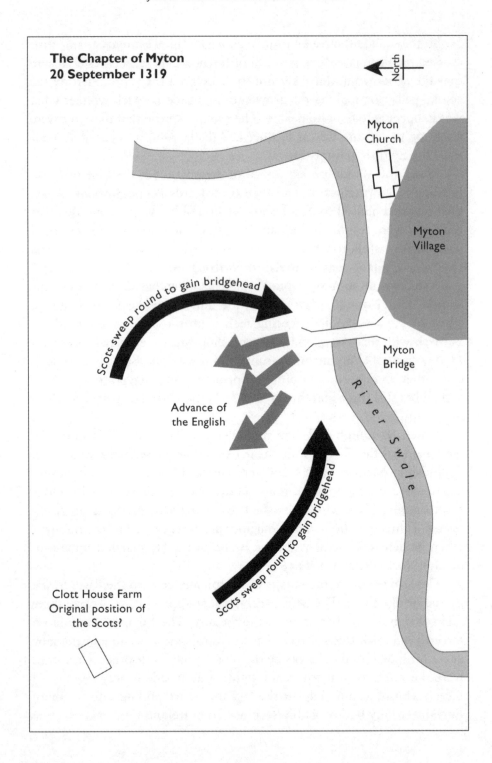

The Chapter of Myton
20 September 1319

North

Myton Church

Myton Village

Scots sweep round to gain bridgehead

Myton Bridge

Advance of the English

River Swale

Scots sweep round to gain bridgehead

Clott House Farm
Original position of the Scots?

At a signal, the Scots let out a battle cry, and it seems the English were suddenly aware of their huge mistake, as the army turned tail and started to run. The Scots charged at their heels. The English ran through the smoke to the bridge over the Swale, only to find that some of the Scots hobelars had galloped round their flanks and secured the bridgehead – their only escape. The slaughter was great, and many of the English leapt into the Swale to try and get away from the mayhem. The Swale is a deep sluggish river and, encumbered in armour or clerical robes, many drowned. The English chronicles say that 4,000 died, and that possibly more drowned in the murky water than were cut down by Scottish steel. The Mayor of York was slain, and many notable people were taken captive.

With a certain sense of irony, because of the number of clergy involved, the Scots called this incident 'The Chapter of Myton'.

Today, Myton-on-Swale is a sleepy little village standing at a road end, situated a couple of miles east of Boroughbridge. There is still a foot-bridge over the river, a Victorian bridge, recently refurbished. Whether it stands on the site of the original is open to debate, one train of though stating that it is slightly upstream, but it connected the village to the fields on the opposite bank. It is possible to park at the roadside by the church. It is reported that many of the slain from the fight were buried in mass graves in this churchyard. From here you can walk down to the Victorian bridge. Cross the bridge where there is a modern plaque giving the details of the battle, and you can walk the footpath round the fields opposite. The Chapter of Myton is known locally as the 'White Battle'. Again, this is a reference to the number of clergy slain, without the irony inherent in the appellation used by the Scots.

It is believed that the Scots' original position was in the area of Clott Farm, and we know that as they charged the English ran back towards the river, so it is relatively easy to picture the scene of the main conflict. The Swale is a deep river, and it is easy to see why so many would have drowned trying to cross its waters. The surrounding banks may have been much marshier then, as modern farming and drainage have probably cleared any waterlogged areas.

A fast rider must have been sent north, for word of the terrible slaughter and the fact that there was no one to oppose the Scots reached the army besieging Berwick on 14 September, just two days later. The northern lords, including Lancaster, understandably wanted to raise the siege at once, and return to defend their homes. The southern English, including the king, insisted that the attack on Berwick should continue. But on hearing the news filtering north, many of the English soldiers began to melt away, leaving the rest of the army no option but to give up and turn south.

Berwick was relieved. James had achieved his goal and succeeded in the task his king had given him.

Perhaps from there the Scots should have gone on and sacked York. After all, there was no one left to defend the place with all the soldiery at Berwick, and the rest of the would-be defenders had been routed or were dead after Myton. Instead, the Scots ravaged the area round Boroughbridge, and there were even reports that some reached as far south as Castleford, on the River Aire just west of Pontefract. After raiding the Pontefract area, this party turned west and followed the river, to reach the other side of the Pennines and then north. Other parties of Scots spilled west along river valleys, ravaging the countryside as they went.

King Edward II did form a barrier to stop the Scots escaping north through Northumberland in the east, but as the Scots had already crossed to the west of the country this blocking tactic proved useless, and they slipped home unopposed.

There was one act of retaliation by the English, although it too proved futile. A strong party waylaid the returning Scots in a narrow ravine in the valley of the River Greta, but after much tough fighting the Scots scattered their enemies, killing Sir Henry Fitz Hugh and taking many knights and squires captive. Pinpointing the location of this fight can be difficult as there are two rivers in northern England that bear the name 'Greta'. One River Greta is a westward flowing tributary of the River Lune, which runs in the vicinity of Burton in Lonsdale. Burton has an impressive moot-hill, the base of a fortification from the time of James. The other Greta flows east just to the south of the A66 as it approaches Scotch Corner, and is a tributary of the River Swale. I have spent time exploring both vicinities, trying to come down in favour of one or the other, trying to locate the 'narrow ravine' mentioned in the chronicles. One of the headstreams of the west flowing Greta flows through an impressive ravine in the vicinity of the much-visited White

Scar caves, just above the village of Ingleton, and this seems possible. But the east flowing Greta has many stretches that are ripe for mounting an attack and it is a route that was much used by Scots invaders. There is more detective work to be done before we can feel sure which place is more likely.

So the Scots disappeared back over the Border. They seemed capable of doing whatever they wanted in England, and King Edward was made to look foolish with his inability to defend his realm.

James and Thomas Randolph were not finished with punishing England in the year 1319. They crossed the Border in force at Gilsland on 1 November. Campaigning this late in the year was totally unexpected by the population of the north west, and this time the raiding was particularly savage. At that time of year the barns were full of the gathered harvest. The Scots took everything they could lay hands on, and wasted much of Cumbria. They raided the lands of Holm Cultram Abbey, taking all the beans and grains from the storehouses.

Holm Cultram was where Edward Longshanks' entrails and brain were buried after his death at Burgh by Sands in 1307. It stands in the little village of Abbeytown, west of Carlisle.

I often wonder what James thought of the plight of the people whose lands he ravaged. At his arrival, poor peasants and farmers would cower in fear. And it was not just the ordinary people who had reason to fear him; the great lords of England knew that he was a warrior *par excellence*. His name had become a watchword for devastation and cruelty. It's hard to believe that James would not have felt a certain amount of sympathy for those whose lands he systematically ransacked. He would never risk a Scot's life needlessly, so he had a heart and cared for his own men's welfare. He had seen the devastation an invading army had done to Scotland, and had grown up with the trials and tribulations that his father had had to endure. He was completely loyal to his king and country, and knew the meaning of truth and the depth of what giving his word could mean. So we can only assume that he wore the robe of a soldier and knew that the course of his life, no matter how distasteful it could be at times, was what was needed to ensure the eventual liberation of his country and its people. That was paramount; it was his whole driving force. He knew his incursions onto English soil were not to subjugate and enslave a people. They were carried out only to force England to come to its senses and recognise Scotland's nationhood.

And he was extremely successful in his endeavours. For one of the few times in her history, Scotland had military superiority over England, even though the latter had 10 times Scotland's population. England's well of resources was deep, and it was something she could draw on to withstand the constant trouble, so James would need to do his job to the utmost to wear her down.

In the *Scalachronica*, Grey informs us that:

> The Scots had got so completely the upper hand and were so insolent that they held the English to be of almost no account.

At Christmas 1319, the English looked for and secured a truce with Scotland. The negotiations took place at Newcastle-upon-Tyne. The truce was to last two years, and obviously King Edward thought that this breathing space would give him a chance to consolidate his position, but all that really happened was that James and Randolph grew in stature, while dissent in England swelled. Much of it was centred round Edward's inability to rule his country efficiently, and James had to take credit for much of that. But the Scots did not tread water during the truce period. They used a different set of tactics to counter English aggression.

1320 is a year that is well known in Scotland, the year of the signing of the Declaration of Arbroath. The Declaration was a letter sent from Scotland to the Pope to try and explain to the pontiff why the Scots were countering English aggression. It is rightly famous, especially for the sentiment of patriotism it displays, and for its call for the right to freedom. The Pope was the most influential figure in Christendom and had long been at loggerheads with Scotland. Bruce had been excommunicated after the murder of the Red Comyn at Dumfries back in 1306, and the Pope had consistently taken England's side in the unrest since, excommunicating the whole country, and both James and Randolph by name. James does not seem to have paid much attention to his excommunication. He knew that the Pope was 'misguided' as to the details of Scotland's situation.

Fifty laymen of the Scottish realm signed the Declaration itself. These included the Earl of Fife, as the senior Scottish earl, along with seven other earls. These included Thomas Randolph, the Earl of Moray. Prominent among the names of the barons is that of James, Lord of Douglas.

The document was most likely drawn up at a meeting in Newbattle Abbey, south of Edinburgh, in March 1320. It is known as the Declaration of Arbroath because Bruce's chancellor, Bernard de Linton, was abbot at the abbey, and he applied the seals to the document and dated it there, on 6 April.

We can assume that the letter and its messengers left from the harbour of Arbroath to begin the long journey to visit the Pope, based at that time in Avignon.

In commemoration of these events, there is a marvellous statue at the south end of Arbroath, on the main road into the town, of Bernard de Linton and King Robert the Bruce holding up the document between them. Arbroath Abbey is a picturesque ruin today. The people of Arbroath are justifiably proud of the amazing document that bears their town's name.

The Declaration begins by tracing the ancestry and history of Scotland and the Scots, some of it fabulous and imaginary, which seems to have been the fashion of the day. It claims that St Andrew himself converted the Scots to Christianity, for example. Where it really breaks the mould though, is where it states that if Robert the Bruce as king did not do all in his power to free Scotland from English interference, then he would be rejected in favour of someone who would, even though Bruce had been responsible for the continued existence of Scotland as a nation in the face of invasion and aggression. Statements like this, advocating people power, are quite out of character for this era.

> But from these countless evils we have been set free, by the help of him who though he afflicts yet heals and restores, by our most tireless prince, king and lord, the lord Robert. He, that his people and heritage might be delivered out of the hands of our enemies, met toil and fatigue, hunger and peril.
>
> Yet if he should give up what he has begun, and agree to make us and our kingdom subject to the King of England or the English, we should exert ourselves at once to drive him out as our enemy and a subverter of his own rights and ours, and make some other man who was well able to defend us, our king.

The lines that echo down the century for every Scot are as follows:

> For, as long as but one hundred of us remain alive, never will we on any condition be brought under English rule. It is in truth, not for glory, riches or honours that we are fighting, but for freedom – for that alone, which no honest man gives up but with life itself.

I can imagine the draft of this being read out to those assembled at Newbattle Abbey, James among them, and the silence as these words were heard for the first time, and what they meant to that company. They have become known to millions of Scots since, but how I would love to have been present and heard the debate regarding this letter to the Pope while standing among that company of veterans.

The Cistercians founded Newbattle Abbey in 1140. Only the crypt and a chapel still survive, and they are incorporated into later buildings. The premises are now in use as a college.

The Declaration was successful, and from that time on the Pope referred to Bruce as 'Robert, illustrious king of Scotland', and took a less jaundiced slant in his attitude towards the Scottish struggle for recognition of their independence.

The two years of truce with England should have been spent in a fairly peaceful state, James getting a chance to act as the lord of his domain, overseeing the day to day running of his estates. But Scots being Scots, there was internal wrangling to shatter the peace. Hard as it seems to believe, a plot to depose King Robert the Bruce was uncovered.

This has become known as the de Soules plot, as the goal of this intrigue was to set William de Soules on the throne of Scotland. De Soules was the hereditary butler of Scotland, but seems to have been quite a colourless character, never appearing to have done anything extraordinary. He was backed by several nobles, mostly of the Comyn faction. Even though Bruce had turned his country's fortune round, there were still those who held a grudge regarding his disposal of the Red Comyn back in 1306.

What seems incredible in this plotting is that the conspirators must have had to consider dealing with the likes of James and Randolph. I'm sure they, and the men who had fought in the many campaigns in England and Ireland since Bannockburn, would not have stood back and let their liege lord be deposed or perhaps even assassinated without putting up a hell of a fight.

But the plot was uncovered, two chronicles saying that it was revealed by Murdoch of Menteith, and Barbour saying that it was a lady who exposed the conspirators.

King Edward II of England was not having an easy time of it south of the Border. There was serious revolt going on in the north of his country, and it was led by the Earl of Lancaster. There was also trouble in the English west, led by the Earl of Hereford. It seems James and Randolph saw the advantages in this trouble, and managed to inveigle themselves in it. They sent secret correspondence to Lancaster, referring to him as 'King Arthur' and no doubt stroking the Earl's ego.

The two-year truce expired at the end of December 1321, and with their customary daring and policy of no time-wasting, James and Randolph raided into England again, appearing before Durham on 15 January 1322. This raiding was on such a ferocious scale that it became known as 'the burning of the bishopric'. They took so much of the food stocks that had been put by, that come the summer, famine began to rage in the district.

The Scots were ready to support the revolt in England, as it was serving their purpose of creating disharmony and therefore instability in the realm. Helping Lancaster and Hereford would perhaps force King Edward to recognise Scottish independence, just to get rid of the added problems that Scotland was causing.

It was a strange turning of the tables. England usually took advantage of disunity in Scotland to enforce her will – the old adage, divide and rule, being a favourite means of control. For once the Scots were able to employ the same tactic, using the unrest in England to try and force their own particular agenda.

Randolph took a force as far south as Darlington, in seeming support of the English revolt. Walter Stewart took another to Richmond in Yorkshire, and James ravaged Hartlepool yet again. The Scots were back in their homeland by early February.

In March, Lancaster and Hereford struck north, and to deny them access to help from the Scots, Andrew Harclay, the man who had defended Carlisle so well against James and others, raised a force and headed south to deal with them. Harclay met them at Boroughbridge, where he took up a position covering the ford and bridge over the River Ure, and on 16 March he utterly routed the rebel force. Hereford was killed in the battle, and Lancaster was executed soon afterwards. A little plaque on the bridge over the Ure in the town commemorates this battle.

Letters were found from the Scots, confirming the fact that there were plans for the rebels to unite with them. Harclay, a seasoned soldier and a man for whom the Scots had much respect, was granted the title Earl of Carlisle by a grateful Edward II.

One interesting point about the fight at Boroughbridge, from a Scottish point of view at least, is that it took place only a few miles west of the Chapter of Myton.

Edward II, heartened by this victory and feeling a sense of security about the state of his kingdom, announced that he would invade Scotland. Word of this decision was soon brought to Bruce's ears. He decided that attack was the best form of defence in this case, and raided over the western side of the Border on 1 July. The Scots went south in two columns, the western led by Bruce, the eastern by James and Randolph together.

During this raid, Bruce travelled down the Cumbrian coast, using the sands where possible to give ease of access for his fast moving riders. He first raided Holm Cultram Abbey, even though his father was buried there.

Holm Cultram was badly damaged by a deliberately started fire on 9 June 2006. Up till that time, Bruce's father's tombstone had survived, and I remember that it stood upright in the abbey's porch. Holm Cultram was a lovely wee place, though not as extensive as it had once been. The remains had survived all those centuries of warfare, only to succumb to modern arsonists.

Reconstruction work is currently underway, so the building is not open to the public at present, but I would imagine that the stone will still be sited in the same location after the repairs.

Strange that Bruce's father was buried in the same church as the brain and entrails of that great enemy of Scotland, Edward Longshanks.

Bruce passed by Egremont, causing destruction in that area, before making his way to Furness Abbey.

The first thing to hit you on the approach to Furness Abbey, sitting in its little vale, is its size. Although today a ruin, much of it is complete to the wallhead. You are left in no doubt that this was a fabulously wealthy place in its heyday. Henry VIII shut it down during his dissolution of the monasteries, and the stripping of its riches began almost at once.

Bruce moved on to Cartmel Priory, and though he plundered the lands, the priory was spared.

Cartmel is still in use today. It has an unusual spire, the top turned at an angle to the rest. It too suffered at the hands of Henry VIII, the domestic buildings being destroyed at that time, but the priory, begun in 1190, is in fantastic condition. All that remains of the ancillary buildings that once surrounded it is the gatehouse of the time of Bruce. It was fortified after his raid there, and it stands in the village just a short walk away from the gate to the priory.

James and Randolph came south through Kendal, and they met with their king at Lancaster. Town and castle suffered there, the Scots burning them both. They all then raided as far south as Preston, bringing back to Scotland as much booty as they could. The supplies would help them during the planned invasion by Edward II, and the devastation would impede his large army on the way north.

The Scots crossed back over the Border on 24 July, with King Edward following them at the start of August, leading an army of over 20,000.

It had come to the showdown. Edward was determined to finish Scotland off, and at the end of the day there would only be one winner.

CHAPTER TWELVE

Beating the English on their own turf

EDWARD'S MIGHTY ARMY crossed the Border around the beginning of August 1322. They ignored Scottish-held Berwick and headed north up to Lauderdale. Bruce knew they were coming and so had put a scorched earth policy into operation, making sure there were no crops, no places of shelter and no beasts for them to find on their road north through Lothian.

I have often wondered at the heartbreak these tactics must have caused. To have to destroy all you have worked for or owned, on the orders of your own king. But I'm sure the folk were in no doubts about the enormity of the English invasion and were ready to do what was needed to ensure Scotland's survival, especially as the English would probably have destroyed or taken all that they owned anyway. Many of those destroying their own crops or driving off their own cattle would have been members of Bruce's forces, making sure their families were evacuated before heading north to join with their king.

Bruce had pulled his army north of the Forth, basing it at Culross in the hopes of drawing the rapidly weakening host on, but it seems James had stayed in the Border area, lying low in the fastnesses of Ettrick Forest with a body of men.

King Edward had provisioned a fleet of ships, and these were to meet the English army at Leith, so his forces pushed on for Edinburgh, finding nothing at all to eat on the way. For three days they sat at Edinburgh, any provisions that they had been carrying long gone, waiting for the promised foodstuffs on the ships. But the fleet had not been able to enter the Firth of Forth due to contrary winds, and some of the ships had fallen prey to privateers operating out of European ports.

The English sacked Holyrood Abbey while they waited. The abbey had been built to house what was believed to be a piece of the True Cross. Longshanks had taken this talisman from the Scots during his invasion of 1296 and it was, like the Stone of Destiny, in London. The abbey was rebuilt after these deprivations, but suffered terribly in the centuries to come, the roof finally falling in 1768. It now stands as a picturesque ruin alongside Holyrood Palace at the foot of Edinburgh's Royal Mile.

Realising that the ships were not going to come, King Edward sent out riders in every direction to try and find sheep or cattle. At Tranent in East Lothian they found one lame cow, and the Earl of Surrey dryly remarked that it was the dearest beef he had ever seen, 'as it must have cost a thousand pounds or more'.

The decision was made to retreat back to England, the Scots at Culross being far out of reach of an army in such a hungry state, and illness and dysentery beginning to take their toll. Three hundred riders were sent ahead of the retreating army. They were instructed to secure the area round Melrose Abbey, to sack the building, and if possible to find supplies for the following host.

It was not long before word of the situation at Melrose reached James's ears, and without delay he set out from the forest to deal with the situation. The English were startled to hear that dreaded war cry 'Douglas! Douglas!' in their midst, and suddenly James's men were upon them, slashing and cutting.

The survivors of this ferocious attack made contact with the rest of their army, and told them that the Black Douglas had fallen upon them. The whole force hastened back to England, crossing over the Border on 2 September. King Edward announced that he would remain in England's north, intending to deal with any Scottish incursions.

Andrew Harclay, the Earl of Carlisle, had left a large retinue guarding the western march in case the Scots had tried to make a raid into England like the one they had carried out to relieve Berwick. These men were disbanded once the English army was back on home soil. Bruce wasted no time. With his army ready, and James and Randolph in attendance, he crossed the Solway and devastated the lands round Carlisle. Taking one of their well-travelled routes, the Scots followed the valley of the River Eden up into the Pennines and dropped down into Yorkshire. Word had reached them that King Edward was lodged in Rievaulx Abbey, and an audacious plan was formed to try and capture Edward. Having the English king in their power would allow the Scots to demand what they wished from London, and recognition of Scotland's full independence for all time coming would be first on the agenda.

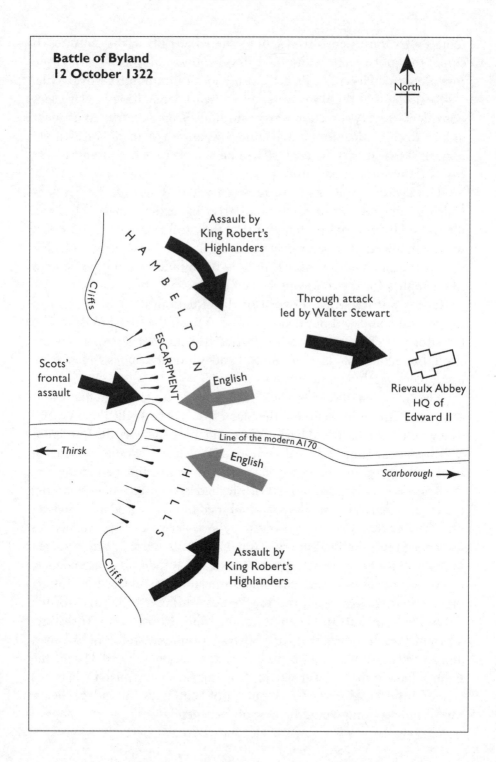

Battle of Byland
12 October 1322

North

Assault by
King Robert's
Highlanders

HAMBELTON

Cliffs

ESCARPMENT

Through attack
led by Walter Stewart

Scots'
frontal
assault

English

Rievaulx Abbey
HQ of
Edward II

Line of the modern A170

← Thirsk

English

Scarborough →

HILLS

Cliffs

Assault by
King Robert's
Highlanders

King Edward was shocked when the information came in that the Scots were only 15 miles away from him, at Northallerton. The direct route through to Rievaulx went up and over the Hambleton Hills, and Edward stationed his forces there under the Earl of Richmond. The Scots knew that they had to risk a frontal assault on Richmond's forces, as taking the longer route round the hills would allow Edward to escape.

The Scots came in from Thirsk, following the line the A170 now runs. On this route the Hambleton Hills loom ahead, rising like a whaleback from the plain. Looking up at the English on that defensive spot, Bruce asked of his captains what they thought their next course of action should be. James stepped forward and said that he was willing to lead a detachment of picked men straight up the escarpment.

Now, if you ever stand and look at the gradient up the Hambleton Hills, and the A170 most likely follows the line of the original pathway, this plan looks to be nothing short of suicidal. But Bruce saw James's brave attempt as a diversionary tactic. Bruce had many Highlanders with him on this raid, and he knew that there was a particular type of warfare they excelled at, and that he could use their ability here.

James chose a large party of men, and made his way forward to the beginning of the rise. He turned and noticed a group of Scots picking their way toward him, and saw a familiar face among them. It was Randolph. He had handed over his own division to another commander and had come to join James's assault with a handful of men.

James stepped forward and welcomed Randolph like a brother, clasping the latter to him. Then he asked Randolph to join him and they made their way up the incline together.

A hail of arrows greeted them as they inched forward, and the English prised loose rocks and boulders, to send them bouncing down towards the Scots.

Bruce sent his Highlanders – Barbour mentions that many were from Argyll and the Isles – to the cliffs that bordered the road up the hills. These men climbed quickly to the top of the escarpment, apparently undetected. They immediately launched a charge into the flank of the English forces, lessening the bombardment that James's party was suffering, so he was able to push on up, urging his men on.

On the plateau-like top, carnage ensued, and the English line began to waver and break. The Highlanders fought like men possessed, cutting their way through the English knights. James and his men, clearing the lip of the escarpment, launched themselves upon their foes with vigour.

As soon as resistance began to crumble, Bruce sent Walter Stewart on to Rievaulx Abbey with a body of horsemen, praying that he could achieve his task of capturing the King of England.

The English suffered heavy losses, and Richmond was captured. Another notable captive was Henry de Sully, the butler of France. James captured him and two other high-ranking French knights. But Bruce would not hold Sully to ransom, and he was eventually allowed to return home. They remained friends from that time on, Sully helping in later negotiations with the English.

Unfortunately, King Edward was warned just in time, and he managed to escape the clutches of Walter Stewart. Fleeing from Rievaulx, Edward had to leave behind his personal possessions, his jewellery, his plate and even his horse trappings. Walter Stewart chased him all the way to the gates of York, and he got to safety behind the city walls by the skin of his teeth.

The fight on the Hambleton Hills became known as the Battle of Byland, due to the proximity of Byland Abbey to the fight. In fact, Barbour thought that King Edward had fled from Byland instead of Rievaulx; quite an easy mistake to make, as the two abbeys are not too far apart.

Rievaulx, like Byland, fell into disuse during the Dissolution in the 16th century. Henry VIII of England had a falling out with the Pope, due to the fact that he kept murdering his wives and marrying afresh. He shut down the monasteries of England, founding his own brand of religion in the shape of the Anglican Church, and stripping many religious houses of their wealth. This was known as the Dissolution.

Rievaulx is a picturesque ruin today, standing in a little sheltered fold in the hilly terrain, and it is open to the public. Byland Abbey, from which the battle takes its name, is in a much more ruinous state than Rievaulx, really only one side standing to any great height, but both are well worth visiting if you are in the vicinity.

Although the Scots had failed in their efforts to capture King Edward, they had defeated him deep in his own realm. It may not have been as absolute a victory for the Scots as Bannockburn, but it must have been more embarrassing for Edward, as he was beaten after a failed invasion of Scotland, and had to run for safety, leaving all his personal belongings behind him.

On my first visit to this battle site, I recall wandering about the escarpment, looking out at the tremendous views to the west, when a local lady asked what I was doing. I spoke to her about the battle there, saying that the kings of both Scotland and England had been in attendance, and telling her a little about the tactics and outcome. She looked at me a bit blankly and said she was a member of the local history society, but had never heard of any such battle. She obviously thought I was touched or making it up!

When I wrote my book *For Freedom*, I spoke about the fact that the Scots still commemorate their defeats such as Flodden and Culloden, whereas the English seem to ignore many of theirs. One reviewer (Scottish, I believe) said that 'the reason the English don't remember their defeats is because they haven't had any worth mentioning.'

So I rest my case. The Battle of Byland is not one that I see mentioned in many history books, so it has obviously just been shelved in the hope that it might go away! And the same applies to another campaign to come in these pages.

Larger-scale maps show some interesting names in the vicinity of the conflict. There is an area slightly south called Scotch Corner, for example (nothing to do with the famous road junction further north), the name perhaps a throwback to the fight.

The Scots took what advantage they could from the situation and the English confusion, and ravaged the East Riding of Yorkshire, riding right down to the Humber estuary before they made their way north again.

The devastation, never mind the depopulation that the Scots caused across northern England in this period, was catastrophic. Colm MacNamee's book *The Wars of the Bruces* gives much academic detail and is a must for anyone who wants to delve into all the hard facts. I quote:

At Easingwold 84 tenants are described as unable to pay the farm. The Scots were blamed specifically for the ruin of 57 of these: 13 had been killed at the Battle of Myton in 1319; nine at the Battle of Bylands in 1322; and another nine killed by the Scots either at Easingwold or at places unspecified. Among these last, one John Baker, tenant at will of an acre and a half, was burnt to death in his house when the Scots arrived there in 1322. Seven other tenants had been driven from the neighbourhood by poverty and destruction caused by the Scots, 10 died in poverty; 17 were reduced to beggary; and the holdings of 17 others are described simply as 'impoverished, burnt and destroyed.'

The constant raiding had destroyed much of the economy of northern England and had pretty much turned Northumberland into a desert, the people either slain or gone further south as refugees. There was no point in their trying to plant crops as the Scots would either trample them or burn the harvest once it was in. As if life in the 14th century was not hard enough, the suffering of the continued warfare on top of all that must have been terrible. If only England, and especially her kings, had not consistently claimed the title Lord Paramount of Scotland, and constantly invaded to try and press these claims, the people of the northern shires could have lived in peace.

The Scots would merely have seen the devastation of England and the taking of her resources as just and fair. 'After all,' I'm sure they would have exclaimed, 'the English started it!'

Meanwhile, Andrew Harclay had realised that his king was never going to be able to defend the people of the north of England, and doing what he thought was best in the circumstances, he entered into a truce with Bruce and Scotland, knowing that it would stop the incursions into his earldom. Bruce went into negotiations with Harclay, saying that if he could convince Edward to recognise Scotland's independence, Scotland would pay the English king £27,000 – a huge sum in those days.

When Edward heard of this, that petulant man had Harclay arrested, and the best soldier in England, who had saved Edward's kingdom by winning Boroughbridge, suffered the full hideous penalty of dragging, hanging and beheading. The sentence was carried out on 3 March 1323. On the scaffold Harclay told the crowd that there had been no hint of treason in his actions – he had only done what he thought best for his people.

Only a few months later, King Edward signed a 13-year truce with Scotland, following the actions of Harclay, whom he had executed for the same deed. Why the Scots accepted this long truce is open to question. Perhaps they thought the English would grow accustomed to the fact that Scotland was a separate entity.

The next few years must have been strange ones for James. He was now in his late 30s, and had lived life in the saddle since he had been in his mid teens. Bruce had granted him wide swathes of land to go with his patrimony of Douglasdale and Carmichael. He was granted Buittle in Galloway, the constableship of Lauder, Cockburn, Bedrule, Staplegordon and half of Westerkirk. He had control of Jedburgh and its castle and the nearby lands of Bonjedward. All these holdings were in the southern parts of Scotland; an acknowledgement of James's sterling works defending the land in those regions.

Life must have been very different for James, taking advantage of the comparatively settled state of the Border instead of living life on a knife-edge, and spending time putting his estates in order.

On 8 November 1324, Bruce granted to James the most famous of all the charters that were to be granted over the years to the illustrious Douglas family. This was the famous 'Emerald Charter', so called because Bruce gifted James an emerald ring to seal the bond. Bruce had released de Sully, and the other two French knights that James had taken captive at Byland, without ransom. James could have profited hugely from the money that the families of these men would have paid for their release. So by way of recompense, Bruce granted James this singular honour. The charter basically gave James the right to keep any funds that arose out of the settlement of criminal jurisdictions, and he could freely hold his castles and lands, unless they were being used for common aid or in defence of the realm.

> And that this charter to the same James and his heirs may in perpetuity stand firm as an oak we have by way of seisin placed with our own hand and the hand of the said James a ring set with a stone called an emerald.

Unfortunately this emerald ring is now lost. It would have been nice to have visited, say, the Museum of Scotland, and to have seen the ring that had passed from the hand of our hero-king of Scots to one of the mightiest warriors our country ever produced.

Because of the truce with England, James was probably able to spend more time with his friend and liege lord, King Robert the Bruce. Bruce had had a galley commissioned, and spent a little time sailing in the

Western Isles. Perhaps James accompanied Bruce on some of these excursions, talking about the early days of the reign and how they had once been hunted men with few friends. They had shared many extraordinary adventures since those days.

There may have been a truce, but stories began to reach Scotland of the intrigues that were taking place at the English court. King Edward II was not exactly the most diplomatic of people and seems to have lacked personal charm. He was extremely pig headed, the situation regarding Scotland testifying to that. He constantly promoted his 'favourites' to high positions in the governance of the realm, and in doing so alienated many of England's great hereditary lords. The relationship between Edward and his French queen, Isabella, was not a happy one, and she eventually took one of his enemies, Roger Mortimer, as her lover.

The King of France had been prompting Edward to cross the Channel to do homage for the Duchy of Aquitaine. Isabella suggested that she take their son, Edward, Prince of Wales (the future King Edward III of England; Edward II had been born in Wales, and his father, Edward I, Longshanks, had bestowed on him the title 'Prince of Wales'. The heir to the throne of England was from this time on known by that title) to France and that he instead be invested, saving King Edward from the obligation. Only after she had left with Prince Edward safely in tow did the English king realise that he had been duped, that his son was beyond his control, and that Mortimer and his queen were an item.

In September 1326, Isabella and Mortimer landed back in England at Harwich with a force spearheaded by 700 Hainaulters, led by John, the brother of the Count of Hainault. King Edward retreated westwards, and he had so alienated the people of England that no real support materialised to help him defend his throne – whereas many of the nobles joined Isabella's banner.

It was feared that Edward II was heading for Ireland, where he might have been able to garner some support, but he was captured in south Wales on 16 November 1326, and incarcerated in Kenilworth Castle. After various machinations King Edward was brought before a court called in the name of Edward, Prince of Wales, the legality of which was at the very least questionable, and there in January 1327 he was forced to abdicate.

The Prince of Wales was crowned King of England, the third Edward to mount the throne, on 2 February 1327.

Although there was ostensibly a truce between Scotland and England, there had been many breaches that had upset those north of the Border. It seems English pirates still thought of Scottish shipping as fair game, and ships had been seized and Scottish citizens killed. Bruce thought it was perhaps time to make the new regime in England aware that there could still be a threat from the north. So on the day that King Edward III was crowned, the Scots mounted an assault on Norham Castle.

Norham Castle today is an impressive ruin, standing on the edge of the River Tweed, its battlements looking out towards Scotland.

During these events, Edward II was held prisoner, becoming an embarrassment to the new power in England, and it was felt a way must be found to annul his influence. It was still possible that he could be used as a figurehead in some future power struggle.

The problem of the deposed king was dealt with a few months later. Edward was moved to Berkeley Castle in Gloucestershire and there, according to Geoffrey le Baker, writing thirty years later, he was murdered horribly. As he was the Lord's anointed, it could not look as though hands had been set on him, so a hollow piece of marrowbone was inserted into his anus, and a red hot poker was pushed up into his vitals, killing him but leaving no obvious marks. It was said that it was partly because of his sexual preferences that the lords who carried out this deed thought it a fitting end. In those days, long before autopsies, it would seem that he had just died of natural causes.

Berkeley Castle is open to the public at certain times of the year, and the room where the murder took place is pointed out.

The disposal of Edward's body became an issue. No one wanted to deal with it, but eventually Gloucester Cathedral agreed to give him a decent burial. His tomb is ornate and canopied, with a beautiful white marble effigy of Edward lying in repose. For a while after his burial, it became a place of pilgrimage, almost a shrine.

I travelled down to Gloucester a few years ago. The cathedral is a magnificent building, with the most magnificent stained glass window I have ever seen. It was quiet, so I was able to sit and contemplate the tomb. I always find such situations quite extraordinary. There lay the man who had been defeated at Bannockburn. He had actually experienced that day and was resting in eternity before me. To be in such places makes Bannockburn and the times that James lived through a little more immediate to me.

CHAPTER THIRTEEN

Masters of all they survey

BECAUSE THERE WAS a new king in England, and a new regime in place, negotiations to continue the truce between Scotland and England opened at York. But behind the scenes both nations were mustering men and preparing for renewed warfare.

It seems Edward III and his advisors realised that because all Scotland wanted was recognition of its independent state, England didn't really have much to lose by reopening hostilities. If the war went in their favour, they would win Scotland, and if the Scots kept invading, the northern shires would be devastated, but they would not lose England.

In June 1327 the talks at York eventually broke down, and the Scots pinned a derogatory note to a church door before they left:

Long beards heartless, painted hoods witless, gay cloaks graceless, make England thriftless.

Bruce himself had business in Ireland. He was still looking for other ways of bringing pressure to bear on England, and so he left Scotland in James's capable hands.

As a warning of Scotland's unhappiness at being no closer to her goal of recognition, James led a raid over the Border. The *Scalachronica* tells us that although a sizeable force of Englishmen gathered and tailed James from only four leagues away, they merely watched as he wasted the countryside in open view of them, so worried were they by his reputation.

As soon as James returned from this raid, he and Randolph decided to do something on a much larger scale. This seemed especially timely as they had word that England was preparing to mount yet another invasion.

Edward III, at the age of 15, was more like his grandfather in outlook than his late father. He desired military victory to add kudos to his new reign, and was amassing a large army. He again hired the Hainaulters, who had helped to depose his father, as they were in the main heavy cavalrymen, and feared throughout Europe. He thought they should be able to crush the lightly armed Scots underfoot. One of these horsemen, Jean le Bel, was later to write a chronicle of his experiences, and his account gives us a window back onto these campaigns.

Edward III led his army towards Durham. They had no idea that the Scots under James and Randolph had already crossed the Border on 14 July 1327 until they saw the smoke of burning villages. Now that James had their undivided attention, he decided it was time to lead them in a merry dance.

The English army's many soldiers were heavily armed and its horses were huge. A baggage train carrying all its supplies and all the necessary equipment to raise a tented town befitting gentlemen wherever they intended to halt for the night followed it.

The Scots on the other hand were riding their usual quick hobins, were comparatively lightly armed, and carried all their supplies in packs on their horses.

Le Bel tells us that the Scots kept iron pans behind their saddles, and when they stopped and lit fires, they would heat these pans. They carried bags of oatmeal, and they would take a handful and mix it with a little river water to make a paste. This they spread out on the iron pans to cook a type of biscuit. As a Scot, I realised that they were making oatcakes, something still very popular in this country.

He also remarked that sometimes they would cut a vein on a cow and mix blood with the mixture and cook that, and this I recognised to be a form of black pudding. They weren't interested in stealing the cattle of course – that would just encumber them and slow them down – but they could use them where they found them for extra sustenance.

The Scots could move so quickly that they easily outpaced the English. James wanted to show them that he had the ability to do as he wished in their realm, so he led them forward in a hopeless pursuit. For two days they chased the Scots 'through woods and swamps and wildernesses, and evil mountains and valleys', according to le Bel. They could not lose the trail, for the Scots were wasting and burning everything in their path. The Scots eventually 'lost' the English by lying low in the valley of the River Gaunless.

Edward III, frustrated, held a council of war, and the decision was made to cut off the Scots' retreat. This would normally be a sensible decision, making your enemy fear for his safety. But Edward was dealing with James of Douglas here, and he seemed capable of making the most of any situation.

The English army marched to Haydon Bridge on the River South Tyne, knowing the Scots would have to cross this river on their way home, and set up camp and settled down to wait. Because it was feared the Scots would attack in the night, they all slept in their armour, and as there was nowhere to tether the horses, they had to sleep with the reins wrapped round their hands. They had kept loaves behind their saddles, but with all the hard riding these had got soaked with horse sweat. The next day it began to rain, and rain hard. The incessant downpour went on for days.

Le Bel tells us the size of the army:

It was said that there were at least 8,000 knights and squires and 30,000 other armed men, of whom half were mounted on small horses and the other half were foot soldiers and light infantry. There were also 24,000 archers not counting the irregulars.

The rain quickly sapped morale, and the English eagerly wished to locate the Scots so that they could bring them to battle and put an end to thinking about their own hardships. Surely if they could confront the Scots with such a huge host they could destroy them once and for all? After a few days the damp became so bad that their leather started to rot and the horses developed sores where their harnesses were rubbing.

While the English were waiting in the rain, the Scots were further south, camped in the rising ground south of the River Wear near the village of Stanhope. They lived much more frugally and had chosen their ground, and did not seem to feel the hardship as badly as their foes.

King Edward III made an announcement. If anyone could lead him to the Scots so that he could give battle, he would give that man a knighthood and an annual income of £100.

Young men rode out in every direction, hoping to win the prize. One squire, Thomas de Rokeby, stumbled upon some Scots near their camp at Stanhope, and he was captured and taken before James. He told him the story of his hoped-for knighthood, and after some thought, James decided to let Thomas go and claim his ennoblement, telling him to inform Edward that the Scots were at Stanhope and were ready and waiting for the English battle host to appear.

Thomas rode back as fast as his horse could carry him, and informed his king where the Scots could be found. The waiting over, the English hurriedly broke camp and marched south. From Haydon Bridge, they would have followed the line traversed by the modern B6303, or perhaps they travelled a little further east and used the line of the B6306. Both routes travel over wild and remote country, and the Hainaulters must have wondered what they had let themselves in for.

On 30 July the English started to deploy in front of the Scots. The Scottish position was most likely on the top of the steep hill on the south bank of the Wear, just opposite to where the football pitch in Stanhope stands today. James would have picked his position well, and the English must have realised that although they outnumbered the Scots two or three to one, the Scots position was unassailable.

James, from the Scots hilltop vantage point, could see much of what went on in the English camp. A thousand archers were plied with drink before being sent out to fire volleys into the Scottish divisions. Why the drink? There is a story that anytime James captured archers he gave them the choice of losing a hand or an eye before releasing them, to make them useless in battle. Although archers were sometimes slain out of hand by victorious armies at that time, this method seemed to instil in them a dread that was unparalleled, and they told stories of James that made him out to be the very Earl of Hell himself.

James came up with a ruse to pull some of the English archers into an ambush. He positioned some cavalry hidden out on the Scottish flanks, and then, covering his famous coat of arms with a cloak, he rode out enticingly close to the bowmen. They took the bait, and many of them ran forward; but Robert Ogle, an English squire, recognised James, and shouted a warning: 'it's the Douglas, the Douglas!' The archers, panicking, started to run back to their positions as James signalled the hidden riders to charge. Ogle's shouted warning saved many, but Barbour tells us that 300 of the archers were slain.

Edward III then sent forward an envoy, who informed James and Randolph and the other Scots leaders that his king was willing to pull back a distance from the northern bank of the river, and that this would give the Scots room to come down from their hilltop position

onto the level plain, where they could fight a fair battle in the chivalrous manner.

James, as we know, would never risk the life of a single one of his
men unnecessarily, and he well knew that he was far outnumbered by
the enemy. He sent the envoy back to his king with the message that
'they were in his realm and had burned it and wasted it; and if this
vexed him he could come and stop them, for they were happy where
they were.'

For three days the two armies sat on either side of the river in a
stalemate situation. Each day there were skirmishes between young
knights, eager to test their mettle in battle, but those captured one day
were usually exchanged for prisoners the next. There were casualties
though, with hot heads getting out of their depth and being slain.

Le Bel tells us that every night the Scots lit bonfires, shouted in chorus,
blew horns and generally made such a din that it was as if the very devils
in hell were let loose. Because of this, the English had to remain in a state
of constant preparedness in case a night time attack materialised.

The Scots noticed something in the English camp they had never
seen before. Some of the English lords were sporting heraldic devices on
top of their war helms – the latest fashion. The Scots much admired these.
Also, the English had been carting about some strange urn-shaped
objects. These were the first cannon that the Scots had seen. There does
not seem to have been one fired in anger during this campaign, which
came to be known as the Weardale Campaign, but early cannon were
unreliable, and perhaps it was the case that the constant rain at
Haydon Bridge had ruined the gunpowder.

After the three days sitting opposite each other, under cover of night
and with the fires left burning, James moved his entire army a mile or
two upstream to an even stronger position.

By daybreak they were settled in, and the English awoke to find that
the hillside above them was empty. It was not long before their scouts
found the Scots, whereupon the whole English army upped sticks and
followed them upstream, and settled down on the opposite bank; a
similar situation to the one that they had just left.

Why did James decide to do this? Perhaps he could see weaknesses
in the position he was in, and knew it would only be a matter of time
before the opposition discovered these and sought to utilise them. The

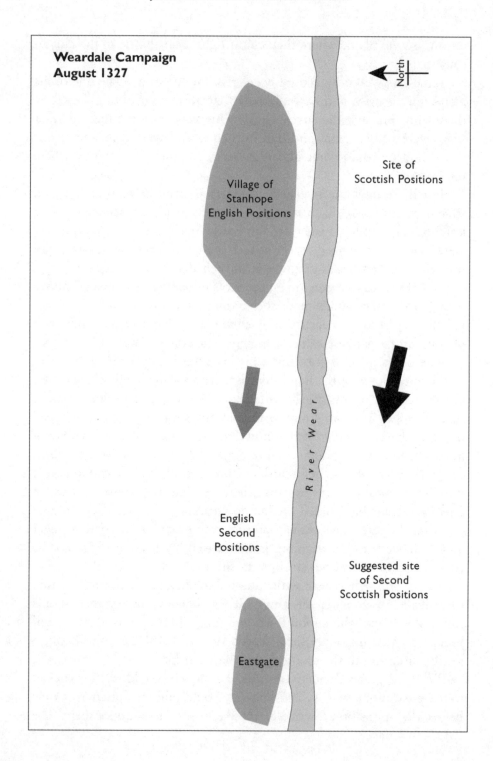

**Weardale Campaign
August 1327**

North

Village of
Stanhope
English Positions

Site of
Scottish Positions

River Wear

English
Second
Positions

Suggested site
of Second
Scottish Positions

Eastgate

Scots' new position in Stanhope Park, a hunting ground of the Bishop of Durham, was more defensible. They had tree cover to protect them, but there was quite a sizeable stretch of bog behind them and the English were soon to perceive that they had them trapped. As far as they were concerned, they could just sit tight, positioned as they were between the Scots and the Border. It would become a waiting game, and Edward could always call up more provisions – this was, after all, his kingdom, and the Scots would eventually run out of food.

But James was James, and being the man he was, an audacious plan had formed in his head. That night, he assembled 200 of his best fighters, all armed with swords and spears. He briefed them. They were going to attack the English camp. They were to cut the tent ropes with slashes of their swords. With their spears they were to stab down and slay the disorientated occupants.

On 4 July he led them out from the Scots camp by a circuitous route, and crossed the river well away from the English camp. Stealthily they approached, and found that the English had not set adequate pickets, so they were able to reach the edge of the tented encampment unopposed. There they broke into a gallop and, slashing, cut the guy ropes of the nearest tents and stabbed at the wriggling bodies beneath with their spears. James cried 'Douglas! Douglas! You shall all die English thieves!' and many woke to hear that dreaded shout. For many it was the last thing they ever heard. The Scots created mayhem in the confusion.

James cut his way right through the camp till he reached the very tent of the King of England himself, its three leopards banner flying outside. He slashed the guy ropes, and stabbed down into the canvas below. Edward's retainers threw themselves over the king to protect him. If things had just been a little different, James might actually have been able to haul the boy-king onto his saddle and make his getaway with the prize that would ensure Scotland's freedom. But James could sense the English were recovering from the shock, and all of that vast camp was beginning to rouse and arm itself, and he knew that the Scots had to make their getaway while they still could.

He blew his horn, and his men, recognising the sound, began to turn and retrace their route away from the camp. James, reaching the edge of the camp, paused to make sure his men were winning clear and that there were no stragglers. One of the English soldiers, more alert than his fellows, had armed himself with a club, and as James turned his horse's head to gallop off after the rest of the Scots, this man hit him with a savage blow, stunning him and almost dropping him from his horse. Disorientated though he was, James, more by instinct than anything else, got caught in a mad struggle with the man, and eventually managed to cut him down.

Meanwhile the rest of the Scots, having reached the crossing point of the river, realised that James was not among them. They stopped and hastily convened. They all loved their commander of course, and as one they decided to go back and see if they could find him, not caring that the whole English camp had been roused. But then, James suddenly rode down to meet them, and told them that he was all right, but it had been a close-fought thing.

The Scots returned to Stanhope Park. They found that they had lost a few men, but it was later reported that they had slain 300 in the English camp. Randolph, finding how well they had fared, suggested that perhaps they should have taken the whole army on this expedition, and that they could have destroyed the English power completely, and perhaps have captured the king. But James replied that he had taken the amount of risk that he had thought necessary, and they had definitely spread terror in the enemy.

Although it was discussed in the camp, James decided that there would be no set battle with the English. He figured that if the Scots could disappear from their positions in the night, it would be a real blow to the English, who expected battle. Randolph asked James how they were going to achieve this. The English were between them and home. They were outnumbered, and if they were seen to be making ready to withdraw, that huge English army would mobilise itself to thwart any move they tried to make. They were in a good position, one that the English could not easily assail, due to the steep ground in front of them, but a large area of marshland defended their rear, and breaking out of the situation they were in without heavy loss seemed impossible.

James decided to tell a story.

He told a tale of a fox and a fisherman. The fisherman built a little hut by a river, a place where he could easily go and check the nets he had set. The hut was a simple affair with a bed within; the only opening was its door, and it had a fireplace.

One night the fisherman went out to see if there was anything in his nets. He took his time about it, and when he returned to his hut, from the doorway he realised there was a fox inside. The glow from the logs burning on the fire lit the scene. The fox had crept inside and had begun gnawing on a salmon, and the reappearance of the fisherman had caught him by surprise. The fisherman, blocking the only way in and out, knew he had the fox trapped, and drew his sword. The fox knew he had nowhere to hide, and desperately looked round the hut for something, anything, to help him escape. The fox noticed the fisherman's cape and hood lying on the bed. He gripped the cape with his teeth and pulled it across the room onto the fire.

The fisherman, seeing his cape beginning to burn, jumped forward to pull it from the flames, and the fox, seeing his opportunity, ran for the door and made his getaway.

James explained:

The English are the fisherman. We are the fox. They think they bar the way and we have no way to go but past them. They must think that after our successful raid on their camp we will be so filled with pride that we must soon give battle, but I have thought of a way to break out. We may get wet, but if we do this right, even the youngest page will not be lost.

The next morning, the English were kept busy gathering up the 300 or so bodies that had been slain during James's foray into their camp. The Scots secretly began to pack up their goods and get ready for the planned withdrawal.

As night fell, the fires in the camp were well stocked up, horns were blown as usual, and the Scots made their way to the rear of their camp and prepared to cross the marshland. They had tied bundles of wood, and these were used so that they could bridge some of the streams and pools.

It took time for everyone to successfully cross the moss. The only casualties were a few packhorses who had got stuck in the mud and had to be left behind.

Once they had won clear, the Scots circled far round the English positions, and made their way north towards their homeland.

King Robert Bruce, on his return from Ireland, was given the information that James and his men were isolated in Weardale, and fearing that there might be disaster with such a large English host stationed against them, had assembled an army of 10,000. This he sent south under the command of the Earls of Angus and March, to relieve James. On the very day that they had crossed the moss and were making their way north, James and his army ran into this host and, not expecting to meet friends deep in England, began to deploy and shout battle cries. When each side heard the other's calls, they realised they were all Scots, and swords were sheathed and greetings exchanged, and the whole company made their way back to Scotland.

Bruce welcomed them heartily and listened to the tale of their escape, pleased that they had raided deep into England, and had faced a much greater army with so little loss of life.

As morning dawned, the English saw that the Scots had disappeared from their position. Some of the Hainaulters tentatively ascended the hillside, to find that the Scots had indeed gone. They had slaughtered the cattle that were in the camp, and had left many pairs of cow skin shoes for some reason. There were leather cauldrons filed with meat and water, ready to be boiled over fires, and this gives us another little insight into how they ate. Le Bel tells us that they found five English prisoners tied to trees 'out of sheer spite,' two whose legs had been broken. They followed the tracks of the Scots and found that they disappeared into the moss, and that they had slipped the noose.

When they reported back to their camp, the young King Edward III wept tears of frustration. He had been shamed deep in his own realm, and had been unable to stop James doing as he pleased. He wrote a letter from Weardale stating that 'his enemies had stolen away by night secretly, as if vanquished'. But these were hollow words. The army was disbanded and Edward III made his way to York to lick his wounds. The Hainaulters had still to be paid, and the bill for their hire came to £55,000. The English treasury was desperately short of money and this almost bankrupted the economy.

Never one to rest where action was needed on Scotland's behalf, Bruce mounted a massive three-pronged incursion into Northumberland only a few weeks later. During August and September 1327 he mounted a siege on Norham Castle, while James and Randolph attacked Alnwick and Warkworth castles, and ravaged all the shire of Northumberland.

But Bruce's tactics had changed in character. He rode round the hunting forests of the area as if they were his own. He started to dole out the lands of this part of England to his own followers as if they were his own domains, and he spent days holding jousting contests, in contempt of the English and their ability to defend their own realm. He also made inroads in annexing property further south in Durham, and even to the North Riding of Yorkshire.

Henry Percy of Alnwick thought the time right to lead a raid into Scotland. With Bruce, James and Randolph busy besieging castles, he reckoned he could waste Teviotdale, and gathered together a force to do so. As soon as James heard of this, he immediately went in pursuit of Percy. Percy heard that James was on his tail, and this news was enough to make him turn back to Newcastle and seek shelter behind its walls. So demoralised were the English, just knowing that James was in the vicinity would make them retreat without seeking a fight.

This upsurge in Scottish activity and display of their power, along with the fact that they were now actually eating away at the realm of England, succeeded in making the regime in London feel that something had to be done. The cost of hiring the Hainaulters had helped the Scots situation too, as the cost of raising an army for possibly pointless incursions into Scotland became prohibitive.

In October 1327, two English envoys came seeking King Robert the Bruce, still besieging Norham Castle. They were Henry Percy, the lord of Alnwick, and an experienced lawyer, William of Denum. They were granted audience with the King of Scots. James and Randolph had joined their king at Norham, and so would have been present at this meeting.

Bruce asked the envoys, what was the object of their mission?

They had come to treat for peace with Scotland.

When the discussions were over, and the envoys had left the room, Bruce must have turned to James and his other captains with a wry smile on his face. It seemed that all that they had fought for over the 21 years since Bruce had been crowned at Scone was about to be realised. It was strange that this incident had happened at Norham. This was the place where Edward Longshanks had gone to back in 1291, to decide who should be the King of Scots. Longshanks' involvement had been the catalyst to start the Wars of Independence. Perhaps it was fitting that the first steps to end that war took place at Norham.

CHAPTER FOURTEEN

Bas Agus Buaidh
(death and victory)

AFTER SOME DELIBERATION, Bruce sent a letter to Edward III from Berwick on 18 October 1327. It outlined six points that Bruce wished to be fulfilled to confirm the lasting peace. In brief, these were:

England must recognise that Scotland was a free nation.

Bruce's heir Prince David should be married to Edward III's sister Joan.

No subject of the King of England could demand lands in Scotland and vice versa.

Scotland would give military aid against anyone who tried to invade England, except for France, and England would do likewise for Scotland.

Scotland would pay England £20,000.

England would put pressure on the Pope to have the excommunication against Bruce lifted.

Edward III wrote back on 30 October, saying that he was happy with the idea of marriage between David and Joan, and that he was happy with the offer of £20,000, but he wished to begin negotiations to talk over the other points. He wrote that if he received satisfaction on these other points, then he would recognise Robert Bruce's title to the Kingdom of Scotland.

Although the English had approached the Scots to ask for peace, the language that Edward used here made it look as if the Scots were coming cap in hand to him.

The discussions began at Newcastle on Tyne and carried on through November and December. Bruce's health had deteriorated and he did not attend in person. He had not been in the best of health for a year or two, but it seems that whatever his ailment was, it was becoming more serious.

James appeared at Newcastle as a Scottish envoy, and so was there to debate the lasting peace between the two nations. He had known warfare his whole life, and now he was helping to bring peace back to Scotland. An independent Scotland.

The negotiations must have gone reasonably well, with a general agreement between the two sides. An English parliament was held at York in March 1328. There a letter was issued, which finished with these words:

> We will and concede for us and all our heirs and successors, by the common counsel, assent and consent of the prelates, magnates, earls and barons and communities of our realm in our parliament that the kingdom of Scotland shall remain for ever separate in all respects from the kingdom of England, in its entirety, free and in peace, without any kind of subjection, servitude, claim or demand, with its rightful boundaries as they were held and preserved in the times of Alexander of good memory, king of Scotland last deceased, to the magnificent prince, the lord Robert, by God's grace illustrious king of Scots, our ally and very dear friend, and to his heirs and successors.

Bruce insisted that the treaty be finalised in Edinburgh, as a mark of respect to Scotland, so the English delegation came north on 10 March 1328. The peace treaty was signed at Holyrood Abbey in Edinburgh on 17 March, 'in a chamber within the precincts of the monastery where the lord king was lying.' Bruce was obviously bed-bound by this point, but James and Randolph were present in his chamber to oversee the proceedings.

Scotland was now a free and independent country. Bruce had seen the realisation of his life's work, and the six points he had laid out for peace had all been recognised. The English ratified the treaty on their side of the Border at Northampton on 4 May.

G. W. S. Barrow's brilliant book *Robert Bruce* makes a telling statement regarding these proceedings:

> If Edward I had chosen to abide by the spirit of that earlier agreement, the treaty of Birgham, which he ratified at Northampton in 1290, the later agreement, which his grandson ratified at

Northampton 38 years afterwards, would never have been necessary, and there would have been no occasion for the dark years of carnage and destruction, and the breeding of hatred between two nations who for the past century had been learning, not without success, to be friends.

Edward 1 of England, in his greed for lands and power, had started a bloody war with Scotland that resulted in many tens of thousands of deaths on both sides of the Border.

Although the English had ratified the Treaty of Edinburgh, as the document came to be known, their kings would later renege their promises and try again to win Scotland. For hundreds of years after the time of Bruce, these wars with England would continue. Even today, race memory means that the two countries still view each other with suspicion. This is the lasting legacy of Longshanks, and it is not one to be proud of.

The marriage between Bruce's young son, Prince David, and Princess Joan, sometimes known as 'Joan of the Tower', took place on 12 July at Berwick on Tweed in the presence of many dignitaries of both realms. James, attended by a glittering retinue of knights, escorted the young princess into the realm of Scotland. Bruce did not attend. Perhaps he was too ill, or perhaps because the English king was not attending, Bruce decided he too would not show face. That means that James was among the main men of note on the Scottish side. He was now famous across Europe, not only as a formidable fighter and battlefield commander, but as a noted statesman too.

Around the time of the marriage, the English offered back the Stone of Destiny and the Holy Rood of St Margaret, the two great talismen of Scotland that had been looted by Edward Longshanks. We are told that a mob gathered in the streets and prevented the Stone's removal from Westminster Abbey. From this time on the English treated it as their own property, and for 700 years it was a real bone of contention between the two nations, until its eventual return to Scotland in 1996, 700 years after it had crossed the Border in the other direction.

It seems the Holy Rood was returned, however, although we are sadly lacking details. Unfortunately King David 11, Bruce's son, carried this venerated object into battle against the English at Neville's Cross, close to Durham, on 17 October 1346. It was an English victory, the Holy Rood was taken, and it was presented to Durham Cathedral, where it remained on show until it disappeared at the Reformation.

I have often wondered if it still survives somewhere, the owner either aware or ignorant of its significance.

Prince David was Bruce's heir, and Bruce, his health fading, understandably wished to make sure his succession was secure. It was decreed that if anything should happen to David, Bruce's grandson Robert, born to his daughter Marjory, would reign instead. (This grandson was eventually to reign as King Robert II, the first of the line of the famous Stewart dynasty.) James, Lord of Douglas, and Thomas Randolph were chosen to be the guardians of these boys if they had to reign as minors. As regent-elect of Scotland, James had reached the very pinnacle of position.

In 1329 Bruce had a slight recovery from the illness that beset him, and although it must have been a terrible strain, he wanted to make a pilgrimage to Whithorn in Galloway in the south west. Whithorn was the place where St Ninian introduced Christianity into Scotland, and Bruce perhaps wished to make repentance for the many lives lost in the wars of the past years in order to ease his soul a little.

James accompanied his master on this trip, and it must have grieved him sorely to see the hero-king so frail and so obviously near his end.

The church at Whithorn still stands complete to the wallhead, and has an attached visitor centre that tells the tale of this cradle of Christian worship in this country.

On the way back north they passed Turnberry Castle, Bruce's birthplace, and Bruce must have looked over the land he explored as a child and reminisced with James. They had shared so many adventures over the past 23 years. They had spent time as hunted fugitives, and had dreamed dreams for their country, and almost all those dreams had come to fruition. I say almost, because there was still one thing that Bruce had not achieved, something he had pledged to himself in his early days of campaigning, and he was to save it for his death bed.

King Robert the Bruce spent his last days at his manor of Cardross, a place he had built for his retirement on the west bank of the River Leven that runs from Loch Lomond into the River Clyde at Dumbarton. The site was until fairly recently marked by Mains of Cardross farm ('mains' here is a corruption of 'demesne', meaning 'the lord's lands'), but it too has been demolished. There are some interesting earthen banks in the surrounding fields, and I have often wondered if they are the remains of boundary walls. The name is not connected with the village of Cardross that stands on the Clyde, nor are the remains in Dumbarton itself connected with Bruce.

During Bruce's final days his friends gathered at Cardross, James among them. Bruce told them of a vow he had made in the early days of the campaign for Scotland's freedom. He had sworn to himself that if he could gain autonomy for his nation, he would, when the final peace was in place, lead an army of his countrymen on a crusade. Although he had achieved all he desired for Scotland, he was near to his life's end, and the fact that he would not now be able to keep that vow, especially with all the bloodshed that Scotland's freedom had entailed, hung heavy upon him. He told his friends that when his death came, he wanted them to remove his heart, and for that heart to be taken on crusade, to be presented at the church of the Holy Sepulchre in Jerusalem, and then to be returned to his beloved Scotland to be buried at Melrose Abbey, a place he was most attached to.

Bruce asked those assembled to choose who they thought was most suited to undertake this last commission.

With one voice they answered him: 'James, Lord of Douglas.'

Bruce replied that he had hoped that they would choose him, but did not want to influence their decision. James then came to his monarch's bedside and grasped him by the hand. This brave warrior, whose name Englishwomen used to terrify their children to make them behave better, told his king through tears that he would do all in his power to fulfil this last command.

A few days later, on 7 June 1329, Scotland's greatest ever king passed away at the age of 55. Future generations would know him as 'Good King Robert'. His breastbone was sawn asunder and his heart was removed, just as he wished, and it was placed in a silver casket, ready for its last journey.

The remainder of the king's body went on a journey of its own, travelling across Scotland, resting at Dunipace, where Wallace had been raised by his uncle, then at Cambuskenneth, near the scene of his great victory at Bannockburn, before it was laid to rest in Dunfermline Abbey.

James was present at the funeral, along with Bruce's other great captains, all veterans of much experience. Did they shed tears, these hard men, as they watched the lowering of his coffin?

A small piece of that coffin is on display at the Stirling Smith Art Gallery and Museum, on Dumbarton Road in Stirling. It is strange to look upon it in its glass case, and to think that James, along with his comrades, saw it on that long-ago day.

Barbour tells us that as the news of Bruce's death spread across the country, the people, not surprisingly, went into a deep mourning.

What was the illness that Bruce succumbed to?

Barbour says that he had a numbness of the body that was brought on by his years of sleeping out in the open, especially those tough years between 1306 and 1309. An English chronicler, writing many years after the fact, mentioned leprosy and examinations of the cast of his skull taken when his tomb was opened in the early 1800s have added some weight to this claim. But we can find no incidences where Bruce was isolated or shunned by any of those close to him, which would certainly have happened if he had had that dreaded disease. It is unfortunate that when his body was re-interred in Dunfermline, it was sealed in pitch, a thick tarry solution, making further forensic work difficult.

His tomb, marked by a brass inscribed with a recumbent figure representing the man, lies at the high altar of the abbey.

Randolph was appointed the regent for the minority of Bruce's son, now King David II, and took over the reins of power in Scotland.

James made ready to carry out his king's last request. He made sure his lands were in safekeeping and under good stewardship, and he compiled his will. He surrounded himself with stalwart companions to lead the expedition. We know a few of the names: brothers John and William of Roslin, William Keith of Galston, Robert and Walter Logan, Sir Alan Cathcart and Symon Loccard of Lee near Lanark.

Early in 1330, James and his men set sail from Berwick. (One later source says Montrose, but as all of James's known companions hailed from south of the Forth and Clyde, Barbour's detail from contemporaries is more likely to be correct.) He carried a letter of safe conduct from Edward III, and a letter of introduction to King Alfonso XI of Castile and Leon, proving that Spain was his first destination. The Moors had invaded southern Spain from North Africa and the fight to repel them was regarded as a holy war. At this time Jerusalem was in the hands of the Saracen, and if circumstances did not change greatly in the next few years, it would be difficult for James to fulfil Bruce's request unless he travelled as a pilgrim. He carried Bruce's heart in a silver casket on a chain that he wore around his neck.

Le Bel tells us that James docked at Sluys in Flanders and stayed there 12 days. He never left his ships, but had kettledrums and trumpets playing on the decks. Le Bel reports that he was accompanied by a ban-neret and six other of the most valiant knights in Scotland, and 20 young squires, not counting the rest of his entourage. His pots, pans, barrels, flagons, basins and ewers were all made of silver, and all the illustrious men who flocked to see this champion of Scotland were entertained with two kinds of wine and two spices.

From Sluys James sailed south, following the coast of France and on to northern Spain. He landed at Santander. I.M. Davis says in *The Black Douglas*:

> During the Carlist wars in Spain (in the 1800s) a visitor to the Basque general Dorregaray had pointed out to him a large grey stone which, Dorregaray said, was a memorial of a great warrior called El Duglas, who came long ago to fight the infidels in Spain.

This episode was described to J. Bain, the compiler of the Calendar of Documents relating to Scotland by Dorregaray's visitor, Count Edward d'Albanie. It is in the introduction to Volume III.

Interesting that he is called 'El Duglas', which is exactly like the Gaelic source of James's name, the stream in his home village, the Dubh Glas or 'Black Water'.

Sailing round the Iberian Peninsula, James eventually reached the mouth of the Guadalquiver, and sailed up towards Seville, the head-quarters of King Alfonso. On hearing of James's arrival, the young king, only 19, summoned him to an audience. The many foreign knights fight-ing with Alfonso against the Moors flocked to see this renowned warrior. Foremost among them were the many English knights who relished the chance to fight with rather than against him for a change.

As you can imagine with men who had fought in many medieval conflicts, their faces bore scars from their experiences. Many would have had terrible puckered wounds, some missing eyes or ears or fingers. One knight of great renown, regarded as being one of the foremost in Christendom, could not believe his eyes when James appeared, his visage whole and unmarked. This man could not help but ask James how his face could be so unblemished, thereby putting into words what the whole company was thinking.

James replied, 'Praise God! Always had I strong hands with which to guard my face.'

Irony was not a strongpoint in 1330, and the company looked on a little confused until the meaning of James's words sank in. Even Barbour in his epic poem felt the need to explain what James meant by this remark, one that is obvious to today's sensibilities.

The plans for the next stage of the campaign were explained to James. The Christian army was centred round Seville. The main headquarters of the Moorish army was at Granada, some 200 miles to the east. Roughly halfway between was the little fortified town of Teba, with its castle standing on the high crag above, the Castillo della Estrella, the Castle of the Stars. It was in the hands of the Moors. The taking of this castle was to be their next objective.

They marched eastwards, and started to invest the town. Siege engines were put in place and the bombardment began. It was not long before word of the siege reached Granada. Forces were assembled, and put under the command of the Moorish general Osmin, a leader of great experience. He advanced his forces towards Teba, halting at Turron a few miles away on the far side of the Guada Teba, the river that runs about a mile distant from the castle.

The siege continued unabated, detachments only attacking the Christians when they went to the Guada Teba to draw water. Alfonso sent some of his men to defend the river, and they reported back that they had observed troop movements. It was realised that the attacks at the river were a diversion, and Osmin intended to attack the camp and destroy the siege. Alfonso kept back the bulk of his army to repulse the main assault on the camp, but sent a detachment down to the river, with James leading the foreign knights.

James gave a speech to his men. He exhorted them to do their best, and to have no fear of death. They were serving God and would have their reward in heaven.

William Keith of Galston did not accompany James on this occasion. He had snapped his arm bone clean through. We do not know how he acquired this injury, but he was most likely wounded in the siege.

James found that the Moors had indeed crossed the river and were making for the town. The whole detachment charged and forced the Moors back across the water. They hit them so hard that they were soon in sight of the Moorish camp at Turron.

Meanwhile Osmin realised that King Alfonso had his army in a state of readiness and was expecting him. The Moorish surprise attack on the camp had been thwarted. Instead, Osmin turned his forces to repulse James's attack on his own camp.

Pushing the Moors back into their camp, James and nine other Scots realised that they had managed to get well ahead of their companions, and that it was time to regroup and fight their way back. James rallied his small group and turned them round. He had the casket containing Bruce's heart round his neck, hanging on its silver chain. They hit the Moors, fighting with all their might, and managed to cut their way through to clear ground on the other side, but then James noticed that Sir William Sinclair of Roslin was not with them. He looked back and saw that Sinclair was sorely beset, surrounded by the enemy, but doing his best to cut his way through to them. James shouted to his few companions, and they wheeled round to go to Sinclair's aid.

Yelling 'Douglas! Douglas!' and smashing into the Moors yet again, they cut their way towards Sinclair with mighty strokes, but the element of surprise had gone and the Moors closed in.

They died bravely. When the battle was over, Keith of Galston and the surviving Scots scoured the field. James was found in the middle of a circle of dead Moors. Five mortal wounds pierced his body. Beside him lay Sinclair of Roslin and the brothers Robert and Walter Logan. The Christians reported that the Scots, on finding James's body, lamented like men gone mad.

Tenderly and in tears, they picked the lifeless form up. Below him lay the silver casket containing the heart of his king. He had dedicated his life to the service of his beloved country, and his countrymen were determined that they would not leave him in a far off land. They would take him home, but his brave heart had gone on to a better place.

CHAPTER FIFTEEN

I have fought the good fight

JAMES'S HEART WAS REMOVED, and then his flesh was stripped away from his bone. Most likely this was achieved by boiling his body. The Scots wanted to take him back to Scotland, but in those days it was a journey that could take many weeks, and decomposition would be very advanced by the time they got there. This was the best they could do in the circumstances.

The flesh was buried in the vicinity of Teba, and I can only assume it was interred somewhere in consecrated ground. James's heart was placed in a casket, and his skeleton was packed up ready to go home.

Bruce's heart in its silver casket had been retrieved from the battlefield, and it too was safely tucked away for its long journey back to Scotland.

The Scots were distraught with grief.

With their cargo they headed back west to Seville and the ships that had brought them on this journey.

James's last battle had been a victory. Just a few days after his death, the castle at Teba fell, and the Christians were victorious.

A few years ago I visited Teba, having travelled inland from Malaga, some 50 miles to the south east. The Castillo della Estrella stands on a high crag looking out the mile or so towards the Guada Teba, the river that James pushed the Moors back across. The village of Teba is on a shelf on the opposite side of the crag. The landscape, dry, sandy and white rock prevalent, must have looked very alien to the Scots, used to the green hills of home.

The castle, really one large square tower surrounded by ancillary buildings, is ruined, but is complete to the wallhead. It is surrounded with two outer ring curtain walls with many defensive towers. Both these walls are ruined, but enough remains to show that this was a place of great strength in its day. I stood on the edge of the crag and viewed the terrain from that marvellous viewpoint, taking in all the places where I imagined the actions of James's last day had happened.

In the square in Teba stands a monument to James. It reads:

Sir James Douglas, most loyal comrade in arms of Robert the Bruce, King of Scots, while on his way to present the Heart of Bruce at the church of the Most Holy Sepulchre Jerusalem, the good Sir James turned aside to support King Alfonso XI capture the strategic Castle of the Stars, Teba, and was slain in battle August 25 1330.

The other side of the monument has the inscription in Spanish.

The monument was placed there in 1988; Douglas Mackintosh, Deputy Attorney of Brockville, Ontario, and his uncle, the Earl of Selkirk, raised the funds for it. It is carved from Scottish granite, and it left on its journey to Teba in August 1988. It has brought a steady stream of visitors from Scotland to Teba, keen to see where one of our great heroes died in battle. Since I mentioned the monument in my book *On the Trail of Robert the Bruce*, it has amazed me how many acquaintances have told me they were on the Costa del Sol on holiday, and made a point of visiting this monument, travelling inland to pay their respects.

In March 2007 it was announced that 173,000 euros had been invested to refurbish the castle tower and create a visitor centre inside. Big changes from my visit, when the only other creatures I saw were a few semi-wild goats!

The ground floor will give visitors information on the castle, the first floor will be about the last crusade between the Moors and the Christians, and the second floor will be dedicated to Sir James Douglas.

James only spent a few weeks of his life in Spain, but the Spanish realise that he is a draw and know to make the most of him. In Scotland so many sites connected with the battle of Bannockburn, our greatest ever victory, along with many other important locations, are to have houses built on them or to be quarried for stone, rather than be shown the respect they are due. A country is the result of its history. Cementing that past with the present day is what makes a people strong and proud. Let us learn from our neighbours, often they have it right.

Sir William Keith of Galston made sure James's remains were returned to Douglas, where James's natural son, Archie Douglas (better known as 'Archie the Grim', because of his 'terrible countenance in warfare against the English'; so very much a chip off the old block, then) raised a magnificent tomb to his father's memory.

This tomb has survived. It is within the little nave of the Church of St Bride, which stands on its little knoll looking out to the Douglas Water. The tomb has been neglected over the centuries. It would have been painted and ornate in its heyday, befitting the man who lay at rest within, but it is weather worn and broken in places today.

The remains of St Bride's were roofless for a long time and the place was vandalised. During Cromwell's occupation of Scotland, for example, he used the church as a stable for his horses, and it was for a long time open for children to play among the tombs, unwittingly causing ruin and destruction, because they were never taught any better.

In the 1800s the Reverend W. Smith wrote:

Last century [the 18th] the school stood in the churchyard. There was no door on the choir, and the boys had full liberty to do as they liked, which liberty they undoubtedly took. So that the ruination of statues attributed to Cromwell was performed by inferior destructionists. I may mention that, though the body of the Good Sir James was brought to Douglas according to tradition or history, no bones were found when recently the space was opened under the effigy.

There is a large burial vault under the floor of the remains, and I have been lucky enough to be present when this vault was opened and allowed to climb down. There are the remains of later Douglas family members down there, but none were interred earlier than about 1800.

There was an enlargement and renovation of these vaults in 1879–91, and many of the old coffins were removed. I have never been able to find out where these remains were taken.

The real truth of the matter is that we do not now know what happened to the bones of James. It is my hope that if they were for some reason cleared from his tomb, they were buried in the hallowed ground round about this old church. He prayed to St Bride, his patron saint, and he was taken all the way back to Scotland by his friends and companions to this little church because they believed it mattered. And it matters to me that he has returned to the soil that spawned him, and I hope his dust is where he would want it to be.

Inserted in the floor of the church there are two leaden heart-shaped caskets, visible under their glass coverings. One is reputed to be the heart of James, the other, that of one of his descendents, Archie Bell-the-Cat (the Douglases were very good at appending memorable nicknames!). Perhaps this really is the heart that was cut from James's lifeless body under the baking August sun in Andalucia and carried lovingly by his companions across land and sea.

A mile or so east of the church of St Bride stand the remains of the famous Castle Dangerous, the place the English tried so hard to hold, and scene of 'Douglas Larder'.

Bruce's heart was brought back to Melrose Abbey as he had asked. It was buried with great reverence beneath the floor of the abbey's chapter house. It was dug up in the 1990s, examined, and then reburied in 1998. The stone that marks its resting place has a heart shape upon it, knotted in a way that makes it look as if it is transfixed by a Saltire, and fittingly a few words of Barbour's:

A noble heart may have no ease if freedom fail.

Randolph had taken over the rule of Scotland, but he outlived James by less than two years. He died in Musselburgh on 20 July 1332. The English had disregarded the Treaty of Edinburgh and invaded. They would never be trustworthy where Scotland was concerned. Randolph had gone south to Cockburnpath to deal with this threat when he was brought news of an English invasion fleet entering the Forth Estuary. He turned back, but his health deteriorated when Musselburgh was reached. It is suspected that he was suffering from gallstones, but the chroniclers of the day were adamant that he had been administered poison as part of an English plot. The ordinary townsfolk of Musselburgh stood guard round the house where he lay ill till they heard that he had died. For this act the place has since been known as the 'Honest Town'.

This house stood till 1809 at the east end of the south side of the High Street.

Of James's companions on his last commission, Sir Simon Loccard was reputed to be partly responsible for the return of Bruce's heart, and there are various family legends regarding his role in the expedition to Spain. The family changed their name to Lockhart in recognition of this, and their family crest is a representation of Bruce's heart contained within a lock!

Sir Alan Cathcart was a benefactor of Paisley Abbey and is reputedly buried there. High on one of the pillars in the nave of the abbey is carved his coat of arms. It is a blue shield supported by two stone lions, and at first glance it looks like three silver ships are depicted upon it, but further inspection reveals that they are three crosses upon three crescents. I can only assume that this is a reference to Christianity overcoming Islam, and recognition of his part in the events in Spain.

The Douglas family changed their coat of arms after James's last journey. His white shield had been surmounted with a blue band containing three white stars. A blood red heart was added to the white shield. Sometimes this heart had the crown of Scotland added too. This is the heart of Bruce, added in recognition of James's last journey and for the loyalty he showed to Scotland throughout his life.

In the first decade of the 21st century, Scotland appears to be finding her feet again. If we look to our history for inspiration, we have giants who once walked among us. Men who gave their all to see their people live in happiness and their country be free.

A noble heart may have no ease if freedom fail indeed.

It just remains to tell you what James actually looked like. For this we again turn to Barbour, who spoke to people who knew James well:

But he was not so fair that we
Should speak greatly of his beauty.
In visage he was somewhat grey
And had black hair as I heard say.
But of limbs he was well made.
With bones great and shoulders broad
His body was well made and lengthy
As those that saw him said to me.
When he was blithe he was lovely

And meek and sweet in company
But when in battle might him see
All other countenance had he
And in speech he lisped somewhat
But that sat him right wondrous well.

So, tall, long limbed and broad shouldered with a pallid complexion and dark hair. Not good looking facially, and he spoke with a lisp. When with others he was charming and good company, but obviously his demeanour was transformed on the battlefield, where it goes without saying that he was a man of violence par excellence. His was a many faceted personality, and he was born at just the right time to do all he could for his beleaguered nation.

James, you have been an inspiration to me since I was a boy, and men of calibre have stood out from the pages of the history books I have devoured over the years. But you are up there with the greats and I hope I have done you some little justice in bringing your story to a new generation.

O Flower of Scotland, when will we see your like again.

Timeline

*For the major events during the life of James,
Lord of Douglas*

1286	Suggested year of James' birth
Night of March 18/19th	King Alexander III dies after a fall from his horse at Kinghorn.
1288	Elizabeth Stewart, James's mother dies.
September 1290	Margaret, the Maid of Norway, granddaughter of Alexander III, dies in Orkney on her way to be crowned Queen of Scots.
October	Edward I of England is asked to intervene and help choose a king by Bishop Fraser
1292	Edward announces John Balliol has the best claim to the throne of Scotland, and on 30 November Balliol is crowned at Scone on the Stone of Destiny.
October 1295	Scotland goes into alliance with France to try and counter aggressive English demands. Through time this becomes known as the 'Auld Alliance'.
March 1296	King Edward orders the invasion of Scotland. The town of Berwick is sacked. The castle governor, William Douglas, the father of James, is taken prisoner.
27 April	Battle of Dunbar takes place. Andrew Murray is captured and is later held captive at Chester.
July	Balliol is captured in Angus and is forced to abdicate.
August	Some 2,000 Scots are forced to sign the 'Ragman's Roll'.

May 1297	William Wallace slays the Sheriff of Lanark. Wallace and William Douglas raid Scone.
	Sometime during the summer months, Andrew Murray escapes from captivity and joins Wallace.
11 September	Wallace and Murray defeat the English at Stirling Bridge.
	Late in the year Wallace invades northern England, and Andrew Murray dies from wounds received at Stirling Bridge.
1298	Sometime in the spring, Wallace is knighted and created Guardian of Scotland at the Kirk of the Forest in Selkirk.
22 July	Battle of Falkirk takes place. Wallace resigns Guardianship.
1299	Wallace travels abroad to France to promote Scottish interests. He later travels to Rome to petition the Pope.
24 Feb 1303	Battle of Roslin takes place. Wallace is reputed to have been present.
1305	Wallace is captured on 3 August and is executed in London, 23 August
10 Feb 1306	Robert the Bruce slays Comyn in Dumfries. Meets James on his way to Scone.
25 March	Bruce crowned at Scone.
19 June	Defeat at Methven.
July/August?	Battle of Dail Righ. King Robert Bruce and James make their way to Dunaverty via Loch Lomond and go on to Rathlin.
February 1307	James launches an attack on Arran and accompanies Bruce to Carrick where the mainland campaign begins.
April	James takes part in the battle of Glen Trool.
May	Another victory at Loudoun Hill.

7 July	King Edward of England dies at Burgh by Sands.
1308	Summer. First raids into northern England.
August	Victory at the Pass of Brander.
1310	Edward II campaigns in Scotland
1312	Raids in northern England continue
1313	Various castles fall into Scottish hands
June	Edward Bruce does a deal with the governor of Stirling Castle, putting the wheels in motion that lead to Bannockburn.
1314	Night of 19 February, James takes Roxburgh Castle.
14 March	Randolph takes Edinburgh Castle.
23/24 June	Battle of Bannockburn
1315	Edward Bruce's expeditions to Ireland begin.
1316	May. Edward Bruce crowned King of Ireland.
November	Bishop Wishart dies and is buried in Glasgow Cathedral.
1317	King Robert campaigns in Ireland.
1–2 April 1318	Capture of Berwick.
14 October	Death of Edward Bruce in battle at Dundalk.
July 1319	Edward II begins the siege of Berwick.
September	Victory at the 'Chapter' of Myton.
6 April 1320	The Declaration of Arbroath issued.
1322	August/September. Edward II leads his final raids into Scotland.
October	Scots raid south into Yorkshire. Battle of Byland takes place on the 20th.
30 May 1323	Scots sign 13-year truce with England.
20 Jan 1327	Edward II deposed.
1 February	Edward III crowned. Scots break truce and raid over the border.

June	Scots raid county Durham.
1–5 August	Scots face Edward II at Stanhope in the Weardale Campaign.
August/September	Scots invade Northumberland.
October/December	negotiations for final peace.
17 March 1328	Treaty of Edinburgh.
12 July	Marriage between David Bruce (later David II) and Joan of the Tower.
7 June 1329	Death of King Robert at Cardross on the River Leven.
25 March 1330	Death of James in battle at Teba, Andalucia.

Bibliography and Further Reading

Ordnance Gazetteer of Scotland (William MacKenzie, London, 1893)

The Topographical, Statistical and Historical Gazetteer of Scotland (A. Fullarton & Co., Glasgow, 1842)

BARBOUR, John. *The Bruce*, edited by A.A.H. Douglas (William MacLennan, Glasgow 1964)

BARBOUR, John. *The Bruce*, translated by George Eyre-Todd (Gowans and Gray Ltd., Glasgow 1907)

BARROW, G.W.S. *Robert Bruce* (Edinburgh University Press, Third Edition, Edinburgh, 1988)

BOWER, Walter. *Scotichronicon*, edited by D.E.R. Watt (Aberdeen University Press, 1991)

DAVIS, I.M. *The Black Douglas* (Routledge and Kegan Paul, London 1974)

DUFFY, Sean. *Robert the Bruce's Irish War* (Tempus, Stroud, 2002)

FORDUN, John. *Chronicle of the Scottish Nation*, edited by W.F. Skene (Edmonston and Douglas, Edinburgh 1872)

MCNAMEE, Colm. *The Wars of the Bruces* (Tuckwell Press, East Lothian, 1997)

PRESTWICH, Michael. *The Three Edwards* (Book Club Associates, London, 1980)

SALTER, Mike. *The Castles of Scotland Series, Five Volumes* (Folly Publications, Worcester, 1994)

Other than the above, many joyous hours have been spent pouring over hundreds of maps over the years, and planning trips by motorcycle to follow the routes taken by armies through southern Scotland and northern England!

Places to visit in northern England with a Douglas connection

AS YOU CAN IMAGINE, when it comes to reading material, I tend to pick up history books, and nine times out of 10 it is a book about Scotland. For me it is not just about absorbing the information contained within the pages, I want to go to the places where the people that I read about and the deeds they performed actually took place.

I think that when you know the story and then get to stand on the spot, you get a complete picture of events that may have taken place many centuries ago, even if that place has changed mightily over the intervening years. Some sense, some air seems to linger, and I can get a better picture in my mind, and hopefully write while seeing the place in my mind's eye.

With this in mind, the following is a wee guide to some of the places visited by James and the Scots during their forays into northern England, places that I hope you may want to visit too. Most of them are marked on the map of England on pviii, and they are all easily located in relatively inexpensive road atlases that can be bought in any high street bookstore.

I get the odd letter from motorcyclists or motorists telling me they used to be hard put to think of somewhere to visit for a drive out, but since reading my books they always make a point of going to a spot I have written about, and taking in the historical scene. That's great, and it pleases me greatly too, as I take such delight in stravaiging about the countryside looking for these places.

In fact I reckon I'm at my happiest when I am doing that. The days I spend that way are the memorable ones, the ones I never forget the detail of, even if I did take a soaking or had to camp in a stupid place because I couldn't find accommodation or the bike fell over or I simply fell off it while looking at something.

So if you do that too (not falling off the bike of course, but going to places for a visit!) I hope you have a good time and learn something in the process. I've always thought that a day when I've learned something new is not a day wasted.

I'll start this at Carlisle, only 10 miles or so over the border into England. It's an easy place to reach, standing close to the main motorway route south. Carlisle has its castle, where the head of King Robert Bruce's brother was displayed on its defences. Wallace was handed over to his escort to take him south to London and his martyrdom at this castle too. Carlisle Castle has figured prominently throughout the turbulent relationship between the nations of Scotland and England. Many stirring or dark deeds have taken place in its vicinity, but of course I'm concentrating on the events of the early 1300s. You can buy a ticket and wander the castle, the old core long predating the times we speak of. The cathedral, which stands nearby, should not be missed. It was here Longshanks donated his litter as he marched towards Scotland and his death, but it is an amazing building in itself. To the west of the cathedral stand long stretches of the wall that James attacked in his bid to take the town. To stand down by the railway lines and look up at that stonework gives me a connection to him, to see a little of what he saw.

From Carlisle you may want to head west and a little north to Burgh by Sands, the spot where Longshanks breathed his last. From the village you have to walk a few hundred yards out onto the flat grassland south of the Solway, but the way to the monument that marks the spot where he died is signposted.

South west of here is the little village of Abbeytown, which takes its name from the abbey of Holm Cultram. Here Bruce's father is buried, and the brain of Longshanks is interred somewhere within. The story is in the *Scotticronicon*. It is unfortunate that the building was recently badly damaged in a malicious fire, but plans to restore it are underway.

On occasion the Scots would gallop their hobins round the coast of the Cumbrian peninsula, crossing the Solway at low tide and using the sands as much as possible on their route south to eventually cross Morecambe Bay and appear at Lancaster. So, as you drive south from here you may want to cast your mind back as you glance over towards the coast, and think of your ancestors spurring their steeds onward, unaware that you, many generations hence, would follow in their footsteps.

Further south we come to Egremont with its ruined castle, with St Bees a little closer to the coast, places familiar to invading Scots.

Although south of here the 595 still bears an 'A' designation, it can be very narrow, and is girt with drystone dykes in places, so travel times are slowed somewhat. You may want to visit the southern attractions of Cumbria on a different day, using junction 36 of the M6 as an access point, depending on your agenda.

Barrow in Furness is the major town, its name stemming from the early iron industry here. It is recorded that the Scots were delighted with the amount of iron they were able to purloin here, and for once chose to encumber themselves with booty. Iron was in high demand to be fashioned into weapons to continue Scotland's defence. Just outside the town is Furness Abbey, an imposing ruin, which must have been a rich, and treasure packed foundation in its heyday, a place that would draw James' men like a magnet. East of here, and to the south of the A590, stands Cartmel Priory, the main building complete and still in use, and in the town stands the gatehouse that was built at the time of James to try and withstand the incursions by invading Scots.

Alternatively from Carlisle we have a choice of routes. We can take the A69 east, running south of Hadrian's Wall. The Scots would cross and re-cross the Wall of course, it probably being a little more of an obstacle seven centuries ago. This takes us to Lanercost Priory near Brampton, the chronicle kept by the monks here tells the stories of Scottish visits. The priory is partly ruined, partly still in use, but all is open to the public for a small fee. Bruce used it as a base, but prior to that it had been visited by Wallace and Longshanks ruled England from here in the months before his death. He built the building known as the 'guesthouse' as his residence, and it was strange to walk past during my last visit and notice someone watching TV within!

Another 20 miles or so further east and we reach Haydon Bridge, where Edward III sat impatiently with his huge army in the rain, waiting for word to be gleaned of the Scots' whereabouts, so that he could destroy them. This was the onset of the 'Weardale Campaign' (see p136). Little did he know that a few days later he would be humbled deep in his own realm by James' genius for warfare. You could, of course, take the line of the B6295 south from here, as Edward probably did, to Stanhope on the River Wear, and to the site of the Scot's positions on the rising ground to the south of the town.

East of Haydon Bridge is Hexham, with its well-preserved priory.

Wallace was here during his incursion, and the Scots visited it many times in the coming years.

Carrying on to the east we eventually reach Newcastle, the Norman castle that gives the place its name standing above the River Tyne. It is intact and open to the public. To the north is Alnwick with its impressive castle, home of the Percy family, sworn enemies of the Douglases. Many fights were to take place between these two families in the coming centuries, probably most prominently at the Battle of Otterburn in 1388. Turning south one can visit Hartlepool, St Hilda's Church pinpointing where the basis of the town was in James' day, at the north sweep of the bay with the modern town stretching away south. The Sandgate stretch of wall on the shore opposite the church was built after Bannockburn to try and give protection from the northern invaders. James, of course, burnt this place several times, and I have stood out on the end of the pier-cum-breakwater here, looking back at the church (one of Bruce's ancestors is buried within) and turning to the sea to imagine the townsfolk bobbing about in boats, trying to escape the wrath of the Scots.

Back to Carlisle, and this time we take the M6 south to junction 40 at Penrith. Turning into the town centre you can visit the ruins of Penrith Castle opposite the railway station. There is no charge to wander round. Taking the A66 east from here we are following a route familiar to James, who often followed the course of the River Eden to its source, before dropping to the other side of the Pennines, very similar in line to this road. We pass various castles on the way, like Brougham and Brough, which were there in James' time. In the village, just beyond Brough Castle there is a little Norman church that is worth a visit too. I often wonder if James was ever inside.

Heading towards Scotch Corner we climb through increasingly rough terrain before dropping over the watershed and following the valley of the River Greta, which may be the site of the repulsed attack on returning Scots.

Further east we reach the town of Barnard Castle, the name of course being self-explanatory. A little south west of the famous junction of Scotch Corner is the town of Richmond standing in a bend of the River Swale. As we drive over the hilltop we see the town huddled round its castle. Its soaring main keep must have been familiar to James on his forays here.

Carrying on south on the A1 gives us an idea of the landscape that so appealed to the Scots looking for tribute and indemnity from burning in the form of cash or goods from the locals. Yorkshire has much rich farmland, and rich farmland produces rich pickings.

Look for the turn off to Thirsk, and from Thirsk we take the A170. We can see the whaleback of the Hambleton Hills rising ahead. At the beginning of the gradient there are signs telling how many heavy goods vehicles have gotten stuck on its savage bends in the last year. On my last visit the sign said 132! It seems extraordinary that James, accompanied by Randolph, could have fought their way up that hillside at the Battle of Byland (see p122).

At the top, there is a car park on the lip of the plateau, and a path to a view-point above the final twist of the road. Here we can look left and right to the cliffs that the Highlanders under King Robert's command scaled to attack the English flanks. On this lip we are probably standing on the site of where the fighting was its heaviest. There is no marker or mention of the battle.

Continuing on the A170 takes us on to Helmsley, where a minor road branches off to the north and on to Rievaulx, where Edward II narrowly escaped the clutches of the victorious Scots under Walter the Steward. The abbey ruins stand in their vale and are open to the public.

Returning towards the A1, you may want to turn a little south to see the ruins of Byland Abbey, from which the battle takes its name. There is a white horse carved in the chalk of the hillsides above.

South on the A1, Ripon is off to the west. The minster in the town centre is where the townsfolk gathered to seek divine intervention to save them from the Scots. It is still a beautiful intact building today, with an ancient crypt below.

Not too distant from here to the south west are the huge and impressive ruins of Fountains Abbey, standing in their pretty vale. You will notice that all the old church buildings you visit are beside rivers in fertile ground, perfect for the monks to grow the produce for which they were famed. This must have been quite a place in its heyday, and it is a shame that its lavish interior and treasures have been lost forever. Unlike English incursions into Scotland, the Scots never burnt these places. They wanted money or goods in exchange for immunity. Our border abbeys were burnt again and again, hence their ruined states today.

Henry VIII was the man who was mostly responsible for the ruin of these English establishments, using religious change as an excuse to seize their wealth and thus began their downfall into empty shells.

Myton-on-Swale is a little further south east, between the A1 and the A19, on little back roads, so a bit of decent map reading is essential. Park at the church as you drive into the village. It is said that many of the dead are buried in this churchyard.

Walk on down to the end of the village where a footpath carries on to the bridge over the Swale. On the bridge peer into the river's depths, where so many of the English drowned. As you cross the bridge you are on the site of the battlefield. There is a modern plaque telling the story of the Chapter of Myton (see p110), a fight the English call the 'White Battle'.

From here you can head towards York, and then cut across country west, heading for Knaresborough, with its ruined castle high above the River Nidd, where James exacted tribute. The A59 takes us on to the vicinity of Bolton Abbey, another place visited by the Scots to exact indemnity from destruction. The priory church stands picturesque in a river bend, the building still partly in use today.

Further west we reach the castle at Skipton, its church nearby, another place where indemnity was exacted. The castle is open to visitors for a fee, and is in a good state of preservation.

From here the A65 takes us back towards the M6, passing Ingleton on the way, where runs the west flowing River Greta.

I take wee trips like this whenever I am able. The line of the hills or the flow of the rivers has not changed much in 700 years, and I get to understand my ancestors more when I follow the routes they took. I read academic history books all the time and get to know the way things happened. Incidentally, I'm not trying to write an academic history book here, and I hasten to add that there is nothing wrong with academic history books! I try to absorb the information I get from these books, and put it together with the landscape and try and tell the story. And I love doing the research. I just hope that you get to enjoy it too.

And just in case you have ever wondered whether your ancestors were 'there'? We all have two parents, whether together or not. We have four grandparents, eight great-grandparents, 16 great-great-grandparents, etc. ad infinitum. You take that back seven centuries; we all have a catchment of 30 million people within us.

That blood has also interbred through these centuries.
Were you there?
If you have Scottish blood, the chances are very much 'yes'!

Index

Some other books published by **LUATH** PRESS

On the Trail of Scotland's History

David R. Ross
ISBN 1 905222 85 8 PBK £7.99

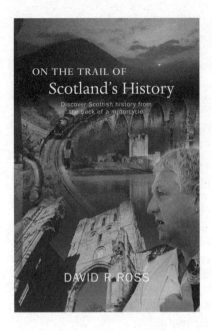

Popular historian David R. Ross tracks Scotland through the ages, detailing incidents, places and people that are key to Scotland's history, from the Dark Ages to Devolution. Leading his readers to ancient monuments and the stories surrounding them, to modern cities and the burial sites of kings, Ross guides us on a quest to discover the essentials of Scottish history – and to find things we never knew existed.

From William Wallace's possible steps, the legend of King Arthur and the reign of Robert the Bruce, to rugged raging battlegrounds, moors and mountains, and Scottish film locations, Ross's journey around Scotland links the past to the present, bringing us face-to-face with the elements that have created the Scotland of today.

An essential read for those who are passionate about Scotland and its mysterious and beautiful tapestry of history and landscape.

The biker-historian's unique combination of unabashed romanticism and easy irreverence make him the ideal guide to historical subjects all too easily swallowed up in maudlin sentiment or 'demythologized' by the academic studies.
THE SCOTSMAN

... an entertainingly outspoken companion for any inquisitive traveller round this nation.
THE HERALD

On the Trail of Bonnie Prince Charlie

David R. Ross

ISBN 0 946487 68 5 PBK £7.99

 *On the Trail of Bonnie Prince Charlie* is the story of the Young Pretender. Born in Italy, grandson of James VII, at a time when the German house of Hanover was on the throne, his father was regarded by many as the rightful king. Bonnie Prince Charlie's campaign to retake the throne in his father's name changed the fate of Scotland. The suffering following the battle of Culloden in 1746 still evokes emotion. Charles' own journey immediately after Culloden is well known: hiding in the heather, escaping to Skye with Flora MacDonald. Little is known of his return to London in 1750 incognito, where he converted to Protestantism (he reconverted to Catholicism before he died and is buried in the Vatican). He was often unwelcome in Europe after the failure of the uprising and came to hate any mention of Scotland and his lost chance.

Yet again popular historian David R. Ross brings his own style to one of Scotland's most famous figures. Bonnie Prince Charlie is part of the folklore of Scotland. He brings forth feelings of antagonism from some and romanticism from others, but all agree on his legal right to the throne.

Ross writes with an immediacy, a dynamism, that makes his subjects come alive on the page.
DUNDEE COURIER

On The Trail of Robert the Bruce

David R. Ross

ISBN 0 946487 52 9 PBK £7.99

 Scots historian David R. Ross charts the story of Scotland's hero-king from his boyhood, through his days of indecision as Scotland suffered under the English yoke, to his assumption of the crown exactly six months after the death of William Wallace. Here is the astonishing blow by blow account of how, against fearful odds, Bruce led the Scots to win their greatest ever victory. Bannockburn was not the end of the story. The war against English oppression lasted another 14 years. Bruce lived just long enough to see his dreams of an independent Scotland come to fruition in 1328 with the signing of the Treaty of Edinburgh. The trail takes us to Bruce sites in Scotland, many of the little known and forgotten battle sites in northern England, and as far afield as the Bruce monuments in Andalusia and Jerusalem.

On the Trail of Robert the Bruce is not all blood and gore. It brings out the love and laughter, pain and passion of one of the great eras of Scottish history. Read it and you will understand why David R. Ross has never knowingly killed a spider in his life.

Desire Lines: A Scottish Odyssey

David R. Ross

ISBN 1 84282 033 8 PBK £9.99

A must read for every Scot, everyone living in Scotland and everyone visiting Scotland!

David R. Ross not only shows us his Scotland but he teaches us it too. You feel as though you are on the back of his motorcycle listening to the stories of his land as you fly with him up and down the smaller roads, the 'desire lines', of Scotland. Ross takes us off the beaten track and away from the main routes chosen for us by modern road builders.

He starts our journey in England and criss-crosses the border telling the bloody tales of the towns and villages. His recounting of Scottish history, its myths and its legends is unapologetically and unashamedly pro-Scots.

Pride and passion for his country, the people, the future of Scotland; and his uncompromising patriotism shines through *Desire Lines*, Ross's homage to his beloved country.

David Ross is a passionate patriot. He is not afraid of stating his opinion, and he does so with unabashed gusto. The result is an enlightening travel book. But beware, it may tempt you on to a motorbike ...
SCOTS MAGAZINE

For Freedom

David R. Ross

ISBN 1 905222 28 9 PBK £7.99

David R. Ross, The 'Biker Historian', goes On The Trail of William Wallace again to investigate his last days, the events that led up to his death, and their repercussions through Scottish history. He ties Wallace's life and death to the issues of patriotism and Scottish nationality over the last 700 years, and identifies Wallace as a 'Scottish Martyr' who died for freedom and identity in the country he loved.

Luath Press Limited
committed to publishing well written books worth reading

LUATH PRESS takes its name from Robert Burns, whose little collie Luath (*Gael.*, swift or nimble) tripped up Jean Armour at a wedding and gave him the chance to speak to the woman who was to be his wife and the abiding love of his life. Burns called one of 'The Twa Dogs' Luath after Cuchullin's hunting dog in Ossian's *Fingal*. Luath Press was established in 1981 in the heart of Burns country, and now resides a few steps up the road from Burns' first lodgings on Edinburgh's Royal Mile.
Luath offers you distinctive writing with a hint of unexpected pleasures.

Most bookshops in the UK, the US, Canada, Australia, New Zealand and parts of Europe either carry our books in stock or can order them for you. To order direct from us, please send a £sterling cheque, postal order, international money order or your credit card details (number, address of cardholder and expiry date) to us at the address below. Please add post and packing as follows: UK – £1.00 per delivery address; overseas surface mail – £2.50 per delivery address; overseas airmail – £3.50 for the first book to each delivery address, plus £1.00 for each additional book by airmail to the same address. If your order is a gift, we will happily enclose your card or message at no extra charge.

Luath Press Limited
543/2 Castlehill
The Royal Mile
Edinburgh EH1 2ND
Scotland
Telephone: 0131 225 4326 (24 hours)
Fax: 0131 225 4324
email: sales@luath.co.uk
Website: www.luath.co.uk